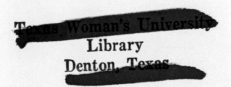

The Montecassino Passion

AND THE POETICS
OF MEDIEVAL DRAMA

The Montecassino Passion

AND THE POETICS
OF MEDIEVAL DRAMA

Robert Edwards

UNIVERSITY OF CALIFORNIA PRESS
Berkeley · Los Angeles · London

University of California Press
Berkeley and Los Angeles, California
University of California Press, Ltd.
London, England
Copyright © 1977 by
The Regents of the University of California
ISBN 0-520-03102-4
Library of Congress Catalog Card Number: 75-22655
Printed in the United States of America

For my mother and father

Contents

Acknowledgments ix

Introduction 1

The Montecassino Passion Play: Translation 10

1. *The Twelfth-Century Passion Play* 22

2. *The Aesthetics of Recovery* 57

3. *The Passion Play and the Visual Arts* 86

4. *The Passion Play and the Liturgy* 123

5. *The Passion Play and the Poetics of Medieval Drama* 159

Conclusion 193

Index 199

Acknowledgments

WRITING THIS BOOK has put me in the debt of many people, and it is a pleasure to acknowledge their assistance. Jerome Mazzaro helped me formulate many of the ideas about the Passion play and medieval drama. His contributions to a theory of the drama are apparent throughout the book. Sandro Sticca published the first extensive study of the Montecassino Passion in *The Latin Passion Play*. His work taught me much about the play and its context, and he has continued to suggest avenues of research. R. Howard Bloch generously shared with me his own insights about the relation of law to medieval narrative structures. Laura Franklin, curator of the Princeton Index of Christian Art at UCLA, advised me on matters of iconography, though any errors or misunderstandings remain mine. A portion of the third chapter, concerning iconography and the Passion play, was previously published in *Comparative Drama* and is reprinted here by permission of the editors of that journal. Francis L. Newton kindly read a translation of the play. I am grateful to him for suggesting improvements and emendations. Martin Stevens and David R. Smith proposed valuable revisions in the original manuscript. At Montecassino, Don Tommaso Leccisotti and Don Faustino Avagliano aided me in examining the manuscript of the Passion play and related materials.

My own interest in the medieval drama I owe to William F. Munson. His teaching and writing first introduced me to the aesthetic and critical dimensions of the drama. With Jean-Pierre Barricelli and Georg Gugelberger, he later supervised my research. All three have given me advice, encouragement, and support. I also wish to acknowledge the help of the following institutions which have made materials available to me: Archivio di Montecassino, Bibliothèque Nationale, British Museum, Biblioteca Medicea Laurenziana, The Pierpont Morgan Library, the libraries of the University of California at Riverside and the University of California at Los Angeles, and the Lockwood Memorial Library at the State University of New York at Buffalo. My research has been supported by grants for summer fellowships from the Research Foundation of the State University of New York. The Institutional Funds Committee of the Faculty of Arts and Letters at the State University of New York at Buffalo, provided a grant for travel to Montecassino. My thanks go also to Pamela Blawat for her aid in preparing the manuscript of the book.

R.E.

Introduction

THE MONTECASSINO PASSION play is the earliest surviving Passion drama in the West. The work was composed at the Benedictine abbey during the middle of the
twelfth century by an anonymous playwright who was probably a member of the order. It is preserved today in the abbey's archive on four severely damaged sheets. For the historian, the creation of such a work is an important development
in the medieval drama. Although plays had been presented
in connection with liturgy since at least the tenth century,
the church-drama focused almost exclusively on the themes
of the Nativity and Resurrection. When it treated the Passion
at all, it saw Christ's suffering and Crucifixion as part of the
scenario for the Easter plays. The Montecassino play is the
first drama to depict the Passion as a complete action in itself,
and it does so without relying directly on a liturgical structure. In this regard alone, the play represents a major innovation in Western drama. In its own age, the play was valued
enough to be copied down, and its status as a text separates
the work from both improvised material and the drama of
popular tradition which it may have influenced later. The
fact that it was not preserved in a liturgical manuscript gives
some indication that contemporaries recognized the special

I

nature of the Passion drama. The play was also important enough to be imitated in the fourteenth century as part of an extended dramatic cycle at Sulmona.

For the critic, the Montecassino play offers an approach to the ideological dimensions of early drama and to its poetics. The play reflects, above all, the essential connection between doctrine and aesthetics. The medieval dramatist could not have discovered or invented a topic more important to the religious life of his contemporaries. They view the Passion as a unique and transcendent event in a history that began with the Fall and will end at the Last Judgment. These concepts dominate Christian thinking on the Passion and shape a distinct view of history. They also provide the critic a set of terms for examining the Passion play. I have relied on them to define what seems to me the central problematic of the work: whereas the Passion is considered a unique and transcendent event, the drama deals with repetition. The very notion of representation implies repetition, and the drama has traditionally depicted events that can recur in history.

The dramatist must find a way of accommodating these different elements; he must synthesize the unique and the recurrent, the transcendent and the historical. The greatest difficulty he faces is to devise a form adequate to the needs of both doctrine and art. Here it is necessary to realize that the play is not the first literary treatment of the Passion. In the early Middle Ages, Latin and Anglo-Saxon lyrics take up the Passion theme. Narrative paraphrases of the Gospel accounts begin to appear even in the vernacular as early as the tenth century. However, neither of these genres presents the Passion directly. Instead, they establish a realm of discourse around the topic, expressing the doctrinal content through the speaker's response to the event. The effect is to distance the religious mystery by focusing on the human emotions.

The direct representation of the Passion requires adaptations that the lyric and narrative poets are unwilling to make in their own genres. For the dramatist, the adaptations probably derive from a process of experiment; by trial and error, he learns which changes suit the dual nature of his material and form. In some cases, the process of experiment involves combining new modes of perception with already established ones. I have concentrated on this kind of dramatic adaptation because it promises the most insight into what the play attempts. The dramatist incorporates iconography and music as strategies for emphasizing the transcendence of the Passion. At the same time, he shapes the action along the lines of judicial procedure and recasts the Biblical narrative in a contemporary verse form as means of retaining the historical sense of the work. In its adaptations, then, the Passion drama emerges as a mixed form.

As much as the topic, these adaptations distinguish the Montecassino text from earlier dramatic writing in the immediate region and in the traditions of religious drama. Plays of various kinds had existed earlier at Montecassino. Ancient Casinum had its theater and amphitheater, visible to the medieval writer as they still are today. In a letter of about 107 (*Epistulae*, VII, 24), Pliny the Younger testifies to dramatic performances by players, pantomimes, and dancers in a troupe supported by one of Casinum's prominent citizens, Ummidia Quadratilla. Contemporary inscriptions credit her with giving the city its amphitheater and a temple and with restoring the theater. In composing a Passion drama, however, the medieval playwright would not be trying to revive the classical theater. If anything, his attitude toward it would be influenced by the views of early writers like Tertullian and Augustine and by their successors, Isidore of Seville and Rabanus Maurus. The creation of a new genre, in fact, brings the twelfth-century author close to the early Christian writers who devised new literary forms and modified the existing pagan genres.

The adaptations of dramatic form to represent the Passion also separate the Montecassino play from earlier church-drama. In the first chapter, I attempt to see the Passion play against the liturgical drama of the West and the dramatized homilies of the East. My purpose is not to analyze those forms in a survey of early medieval drama but to provide a contrast for the later work. Through that contrast, it becomes apparent that a new approach to representation underlies the Passion play. The liturgical plays depend on the cyclicism and repetition of ritual. From the very start, the distinction between audience and participant in them is unclear, and it is through this ambiguity that the liturgical dramatist allows the illusion that Biblical events are being reenacted. In the dramatized homilies of the East, representation has a formal rhetorical basis. The kontakia do not offer a ritual enactment of Biblical scenes, but they do use oratory to evoke images of the Scriptural narrative and to direct the audience's emotions.

In choosing to create a new dramatic form, the dramatist would be choosing as well to follow aesthetic principles that diverge from those which inform earlier works. These changes have their sources in religious doctrine, but they do not occur in isolation from a social context. By its very nature, the drama is a social form. The second chapter deals with the connection between the aesthetics of the Passion Play and one of Montecassino's preoccupations during the eleventh and twelfth centuries. The possibility I want to explore is that the play's dual focus on transcendence and history may be related to a special interest in the Christian past. Contemporary writing and other aspects of social life at the abbey show the development of a Christian antiquarianism. The Cassinesi return consciously to models in the Bible, church history, and the monastery's own past; and they give a particular emphasis to the imaginative treatment of earlier events and locales. In this respect, both the Passion play and the social values aim to recover elements of history, and one can see the antiquarianism as a complement to the aesthetics imposed on the play by its topic.

The third chapter examines the relation of the Montecassino text to the visual arts. The manuscript itself provides a rationale for such a study. Its original plan included a group of miniatures, either as an embellishment to the text or as a guide for later productions of the play. By linking his work to the visual arts, the playwright would achieve several effects. Medieval theories of religious art assert the power of images to represent transcendent events. To the degree that the play uses established iconographical programs, it becomes a counterpart to church art and so inherits its power. The relation extends, however, beyond the analogy of art and drama to influence the visual character and the acceptance of the play. The iconographical programs offer the dramatist specific models for executing the scenes of the Biblical narrative. The extent and nature of his reliance on these visual models are complex matters. At times, he seems to prefer the traditions of miniature art to the details of the original narrative. In tracing the visual sources, I have stressed the place of Byzantine miniature cycles, although there is reference to works of different provenance. The many ties between Montecassino and Byzantium in this period suggest that the surviving miniatures might offer the best examples of the works to which the dramatist had access. The conventionality of the cycles offers some assurance of their reliability. It also proves valuable in the author's attempt to establish the conventions of the new genre. Since the visual element of the work is familiar, the audience can accept other innovations by the playwright.

The fourth chapter tries to make a fundamental distinction between liturgy and drama. For over a century, critics have discussed the ties between the two forms. At base, the issue is to separate the dramatic from the drama. Although the Mass and other liturgical observances may have dramatic elements, they are not drama in themselves. Historians and theorists of the form point out that liturgy is viewed as transcendent. By contrast, drama retains its historical and social nature. As the Passion play demonstrates, even when it deals with transcendent matters, the drama remains committed to a specific audience. From this distinction, we can assess the differences between the Mass and the Passion play and deal with the relatively late appearance of the Passion drama as a representation of mystery. It also becomes possible to examine why the drama incorporates liturgical music into its structure. Finally, by a study of the monastic offices for Good Friday, one can define the relation of the Passion drama to its immediate liturgical context.

The Passion play's concern with transcendent action is an emphasis that remains alien to our expectations of the drama. However, other elements of the work are accessible to the modern audience and reader. The fifth chapter returns to these elements and their impact on critical thinking about the medieval drama. The techniques of staging the Passion play come closest to what we might accept as theatrical conventions. Like the modern director, the twelfth-century playwright deals with matters of exposition and stage movement. To a degree, then, the work can be approached through a modified Aristotelian system; but the modifications must take into account the traditional attitudes of Christian writers toward classical tragedy. Those writers redefine spectacle and make it an essential part of Christian drama. The category of character, which Aristotle subordinates to plot, becomes primary; and the choices made by characters determine the thought (*dianoia*) of the play. These modifications do not represent a medieval dramatic theory; rather, they develop in a process that begins with St. Paul's concept of spectacle and continues through the commentators and early playwrights.

In discussing the Montecassino play, I have tried to stress its differences from earlier and later forms. Aristotle describes a drama based on logic; its patterns and characters can be defined through induction and observation. Consequently, the action of tragedy can be repeated in history, though the moral aim of tragedy is to forestall such repetition. In this respect, classical tragedy is the antithesis of a drama that portrays unique events. Later medieval Passion plays offer another contrast to the Montecassino play. My aim in mentioning them is not to trace the rhetorical development of the form. I want only to point out the changes in their conventions. The English mystery cycles treat the Passion in a larger framework that emerges without influence from the Montecassino play. Whereas the earlier work concentrates solely on the Passion sequence, the mystery cycles view the Passion in its historical relation to the Fall and the Redemption. In addition, they are much more direct in calling attention to the lessons of that history.

Despite these changing conventions, the Montecassino Passion reflects the new purposes that medieval drama gives to imitation. On one level, the play directs material representation to its ideal counterpart. By a kind of sympathetic movement, the exterior forms of events reenacted in the play invoke the unique and transcendent. On another level, imitation is directed toward the audience. The depiction of the Passion sequence sets out the alternatives of moral choice that also exist for the viewers in their own lives. Although the play does not urge reform, it continually images the choices of faith and disbelief. As this empathetic feature combines with the sympathetic movement, the drama becomes something of a paradigm of figural truth. Its sense of spectacle establishes a continuum between religious mystery and the social functions of imitation. Later medieval plays give a different relative weight to the religious and social elements, but they retain the connection. The Montecassino Passion thus offers an approach to the poetics of medieval drama. It is a test case for dramatic and literary criticism.

Finally, the concept of imitation extends to what might be described as the textuality of the play. There is a natural inclination to equate the play acted in the twelfth century with the manuscript preserved in the archive. Pressed too far, such an equation obscures the special nature of both the play and the text. Spectacle, as Aristotle rightly observes, is the most ephemeral part of the drama; and the actual play stands beyond recovery. The text, however, remains as a document of the play. Its combination of rubrics and speeches defines not only the shape of the drama but also the intentions that go into producing the work. An independent grammar of representation underlies the rubrics and the speeches that the characters deliver in performance. Thus the text is pre-dramatic; it imitates the idea of a Passion play. The translation offered here attempts to render this quality of textuality. It tries to convey the optative, speculative sense of the prose directions. At the same time, it tries to retain the sense of a highly formalized diction in the speeches, although the original verse is given as prose. As script and as document, the Montecassino text realizes the scope of possibilities implied by the titles of two later German pieces—*ludus de passione*, 'a play about the Passion.'

The Montecassino Passion Play

TRANSLATION

[vv. 1–33. JUDAS' BARGAIN]

Let Judas say:
> Greetings to you, priests. The gifts of character and the glory of virtue enhance you.

Let Caiaphas answer Judas and say:
> Greetings to you, brother Judas. Tell us what you want now, seeking our doorway.

and let Judas reply to Caiaphas:
> Jesus, the author of deceit, the usurper of our people with his loathsome, guileful name. By now he has seduced many of our people; he won them over into error by a deceitful claim. If he continues living, all the people will go astray because of his seductive counsel. I shall turn him over to you if you wish to pay appropriately for my works.

Let Caiaphas answer this and tell him:
> If you do what you say, then you will get whatever you ask from us. If you carry out what we ask, we shall give you thirty silver coins of full weight.

Then let Caiaphas give the silver coins to Judas, and let Judas say to the priests:

Hurry the deed and give me some followers who are loyal and quick.

and let Caiaphas instruct the armed men to go with Judas and let him say:

Lead these best retainers, all heavily armed, as your comrades.

Then let Judas go out with the armed men and, holding council with them, let him go to the place where Jesus is praying and let him say:

Take this for a sign—cautiously seize the man whom I shall now kiss.

[vv. 34–51. THE BETRAYAL AND ARREST]

Then let Judas go to that place where Jesus is praying, just as it is written above. and let Judas say in a loud voice, bending toward him and kissing this Jesus and let him say:

Hail, teacher of truth, etc.

Hail, teacher of truth in whom no one finds the smallest measure of deceit.

and let Jesus answer Judas and say to him:

Why have you come, friend? You have come out with me secretly to destroy me like a thief. Why did you men not seize me when you used to see me stand teaching in the temple? Coming with lanterns, weapons, clubs, and lamps, tell me whom you seek.

Let the armed men answer this in a loud voice and say:

Jesus the man from Nazareth, the man of innumerable frauds and ghastly faults.

Then let Jesus reply to the armed men and say to them:

If I am the one you seek, let those go whom you see with me.

[vv. 52–69]

When these things are said, let the armed men take Jesus and bind him and let the disciples flee. and let Peter strike off Malchus' ear, saying:

But why, wretch, you spiteful thing,* why do you shoot these deceitful words like poisoned darts? You want to seize the teacher; now I'll make you deaf.

Let the Lord Jesus say to Peter:

You are clearly wrong now, Peter. Put the sword you brandished back into the scabbard. For whoever wields a sword will finally perish by it. That is not in doubt. And yet if I should ask the Father, I would see more than twelve battle-columns of angels. Thus the true Scripture, the true sayings, and testimony of the prophets are fulfilled.

[vv. 70–102. CHRIST BEFORE CAIAPHAS]

Then let the armed men lead Jesus bound to the priests. During the time they lead him, let them say in a loud voice:

Look, we have Jesus whom we lead bound into the courtyard of Caiaphas where the leaders of the people, the scribes, and elders hold council.

Then while Jesus stands bound before the priests, let two men rise up from the other armed soldiers and cry against him, saying:

Hear us.

Hear us, you people standing around here, for we are giving true testimony. He said he was going to destroy the temple of God and rebuild it after three days.

---

* Inguanez reconstructs v. 52 as "[S]et [cur] nequam re[t]exosa." The form *retexosa* is unattested, so far as I know, and I have construed it as *res exosa*, 'you spiteful thing.' I am grateful to Professor Francis Newton for suggesting this emendation.

Let Jesus make no response to this but let Caiaphas cry against him and say:

You say nothing to the charges? These are not contrived words; this is not a lie. We beseech you by God and ask you if you are the son of God.

Then let the Lord Jesus answer Caiaphas and say:

The man you see listening here you will also see coming in heavenly clouds, and you will see the mighty son of God sitting at the right hand of power.

Then let Caiaphas cry against Jesus in a loud voice and rend his own garments and rise up from the throne and strike himself and say:

He blasphemed. Why are we silent? Why do we bother with witnesses? Look, I tear the tunic.

Then let the armed men answer against Jesus in a loud voice and let them strike him and spit in his face and say:

Let the defendant be put to death. Let his neck bow under the blows. What is this he said? Prophesy to us now, Christ; tell us who just hit you.

[vv. 103–126. PETER'S DENIAL]

While these things written above are being done and while the false witnesses are accusing Jesus before Caiaphas, let the maid cry against Peter and say:

You were with Jesus the Galilean. I say you were with him. I saw you without a doubt.

and let Peter answer the maid and say:

I truly do not know what you are talking about. Why do you weave together false words to create a foul lie?

and a second time let the maid come to Peter and say to him:

Were you not with the Nazarene? I say in all sincerity that you were. Why are you hiding it from us?

and let Peter deny again and say:

I call on God as my witness that I do not know the man. I do not know what you are talking about.

Then let the maid come again and cry against Peter and say:

Although it is annoying to you, your accent exposes you and gives you away.

and let Peter deny a third time and swear and say:

I swear in the name of truth that I do not know what you are talking about . . . completely false.

At this point let the rooster crow and let Jesus look at Peter. Then . . . before Caiaphas. and let Peter lament and go to the disciples who remain in hiding and let him say:

Oh, how deeply I have sinned. Three times I denied Jesus and now the cock has crowed. Look, I cry bitterly now. My tongue denied him whom I had promised to love.

[vv. 127–138. JUDAS' REPENTANCE]

During this time let Jesus be taken from the presence of Caiaphas and let them lead him bound before Pilate, saying:

Let us lead Jesus tightly bound to Pilate, ruler of the Jews. Let us bind Jesus to a pillar, sinking to his ruin, a hostage to death.

Also while Peter is lamenting, let Judas carry back the coins and throw them on a table in front of Caiaphas, crying and saying:

Look, I have brought back the coins. Oh, how deeply I have sinned, betraying righteous blood.

To this let Caiaphas answer Judas:

What is that to us? It is your concern. You will get nothing else now. We have the man now.

and let Annas take back the coins from Judas and say:

Let the treasure of the temple not be fee money; instead

let it be a gift for the potter's field. It is the price of blood.
In that field let foreigners who have come to the end of
their lives receive a grave.

[vv. 139–171. THE TRIAL BEFORE PILATE]

and Judas goes out and hangs himself. Meanwhile let the
armed men lead Jesus bound before Pilate, saying:

Let us lead Jesus tightly bound to Pilate, ruler of the Jews.
Let us bind Jesus to the pillar, sinking to his ruin, a hostage
to death.

After this let the soldiers holding the bound Jesus kneel and
say to Pilate:

Hail, famous protector. Rejoice always in good fortune,
most kind protector.

and let Pilate respond to the soldiers and say:

Brothers, welcome. What is that you are carrying? Speak
quickly.

and let the soldiers say:

Look, the priests send you the foul seducer of our people.
They ask and desire that he be hanged from a cross and be
fixed to it with nails. He said he was a king. Challenging
Caesar, he must die.

Then let Pilate say to the Lord Jesus:

Are you indeed the king of the Jews? The voices of those
who gravely accuse you are numberless.

And let Jesus reply to Pilate and say:

I do not deny what you said. I am the king of the Jews.
You speak truly.

Then let the priests and soldiers cry against Jesus and say:

Crucify him, good protector. This man who sins so gravely
should rightly die.

and let Pilate say to the Lord Jesus:

15

Do you not hear what they are saying now? How much witness these men bear against you.

[vv. 172–228. PROCULA'S DREAM]

Let Jesus answer nothing to this but be taken from the presence of Pilate while his wife sleeps, and he is tied to a pillar and let him be whipped. and let Jesus stand bound until the maid returns from Pilate.

While the things written above are being done all the while that Jesus stands bound to the pillar let Pilate's wife sleep. and let a devil appear to her as she sleeps in her dreams. Let the wife of Pilate say to the maid:

Stop the delays and hurry. Say to my husband, "Turn away," lest he harm an innocent person. Let him not bother that just man, sublime in his miracles, a magnificent prophet. On account of him I am very weary, and I was disturbed by many different troubles in my sleep. Last night, troubled by visions, I did not sleep as I usually do.

Then let the maid go to Pilate and greet him and say:

Pilate, famous protector, you are distinguished in your noble character. Lend your ears to this.

and let Pilate answer the maid and say:

I shall lend my ears to you. But make sure I find favorable things come forward.

and let the maid answer Pilate and say to him:

Your beautiful, gracious, and foreseeing wife Procula sends me to you. Now while she was asleep it happened that she suffered serious dangers. When she had given herself over to rest, seeing dreadful things, she did not find repose. She saw many visions, apparitions, and horrible dreams. Thus faithful to you, she asks that you fulfill your vows to her

16

and give her this favor. Do not hurt that man, righteous and firm in goodness. Do not hurt the man.

and let Pilate answer the maid and say to her:
Go, announce to my wife that I will not compel the man to die nor will I shed his blood.

Then let the maid return to Pilate's wife and say to her:
Why do you linger there like a block of wood?* You are sad and pale and speak in such a low voice. Rejoice greatly because what you commanded through me has been done fittingly. Your husband admitted that not freely but against his will he conducts that court. With a tranquil expression, he answered that by no means would he inflict injury on the Nazarene.

Then let Pilate's wife raise her hands to heaven and say:
Praised be the name of God because the ruler will not be stained by righteous blood.

and let Pilate's wife order the maid and say to her:
Go, sit with the servants and work with them now, weaving a full distaff.

[vv. 229–273. THE TRIAL BEFORE PILATE]

Then let the wife of Pilate and the maid retire. Then let Jesus be freed from the column and be brought before Pilate and let Pilate say to him:
I wonder very much at your being silent and never replying to such serious charges. Do you not wish to reply to me whom you see commanding this court and who holds you

---

* The MS gives the form *stipida*, which seems to be unattested. If it is the word intended, then it must have a meaning like the one I have given it from *stipes*, 'log, stock, trunk.' The other possibility is a scribal error for *stupida*, 'senseless, confounded, amazed.'

bound in chains? Do you not know that I have the power
of releasing or killing you?

Let Jesus answer Pilate and say to him:

You would not have power or control over me unless this
divine power were bestowed on you from above and given
from heaven.

*Then let Pilate rise up and say to the priests and soldiers in a
loud voice:*

Which one do you want released to you—Barabbas or
Jesus, condemned by many witnesses?

and let the soldiers answer against Jesus and say:

Let this man Jesus be crucified, but let Barabbas be set free
by the people's petition.

Then let the priests say:

If this enemy is spared, you are not a friend of Caesar.
Ruler, be warned. Whoever says he is a king challenges
Augustus. That is what this wretched man did.

Then let Pilate reply to the priests:

What am I going to do about Jesus? What decision am I to
render over him? Give me your advice.

*and let the priests stretch out their hands against Jesus and
say in a loud voice:*

Crucify him, crucify him. Strike him with many punishments, protector, this most vile man.

*With this let Pilate rise and wash his hands before everyone,
saying:*

Let his blood not touch me. I am innocent of his death, and
my hands are washed.

Then let the priests answer in a loud voice and say:

Let this blood pour out on us. Let us not be spared the
charge, or our successors.

Then let Pilate give Jesus bound by a rope to the priests; let him say to them:

Look at Jesus scourged. I give him to you condemned. Go, crucify him. Barabbas has been released to you, but let Jesus be crucified. Do as you will.

[vv. 274–291]

Then let the priests and soldiers take Jesus and lead him to another place and take off his garments and let them say:

Let this Jesus be stripped of his clothing and let him put on a scarlet robe. Let us honor him on our knees and let us wreathe him with a crown of thorns. Let us mock him greatly, spit in his face, putting a reed in his right hand.

Here let them put the reed in Jesus' hand and spit in his face and say:

Let us punish Jesus harshly. Let us beat and strike his brow back and front.

Here let them put the purple on him and put the crown of thorns on his head and the reed, and kneeling let the armed men say:

Hail now, king of the Jews. Hail, glory of the angels, holding a reed in your right hand.

and immediately afterward let them cry, saying:

But . . . let us not delay . . . and let us crucify Jesus on Mount Calvary.

[vv. 292–317]

Then let the armed men divest Jesus of his cloak and dress him in his own vestments and lead him to the place where he is going to be crucified . . . on his neck and let them fashion . . .

the cross. Let the Lord Jesus kneel and raise his hands to heaven; praying for the Jewish crucifiers, he says in a loud voice:

. . . .

Then let Jesus rise from the ground and let the soldiers unclothe him . . . let them put him on the cross and two robbers . . . on the cross. Let the soldiers divide Christ's garments and say:

Let lots be cast for his clothes so that into parts. . . .

. . . *and Caiaphas standing before the cross shake their heads:*
Oh, you who were going to wreck and rebuild the same temple in three days. Let him escape from the cross . . . Let him save himself from the punishment of the cross.

. . . *let him reply. These things said, let the priests go back to their places and . . . standing some distance off . . . and let him tear his clothes . . . and let them speak against Jesus. Let one of the two crucified robbers cry out against Jesus and say:*
You said you were Christ. Save yourself and me and this one, rescuing us from the punishment.

and let the other robber say:
What did you say, miserable thief? We deserve to be tortured under a black judgment. Are you not afraid of the true God? Do you not recognize that you are guilty under the same sentence? We are condemned by proper law but this one, what has he done to suffer such harsh punishment?

and continuing on let the robber say to Jesus:
Lord, remember me when you shall come to the kingdom of God where you rule forever.

and let Jesus answer him and say:
Amen, I say to you, thief, you will come with me today into holy paradise.

[vv. 318–320]

... the mother ... standing with John and the other women before the cross ... toward him ... as if showing him the womb in which she carried Christ. When the blessed Virgin, grieving because he does not speak at all to the thief who talked to him and to his own weeping mother, this blessed Virgin calls out to her crucified son with a powerful cry, and says before the armed men:

... Why did I carry you in my womb, when I see you dying now. Remember me in your kingdom.

1. The Twelfth-Century Passion Play

IN 1936 Dom Mauro Inguanez published the text of a Montecassino Passion play.[1] The fragmentary drama is the earliest surviving example of a Latin Passion play. It dates to the middle of the twelfth century and was rebound in the *Registrum I Thomae Abbatis 1285–1288*. The present text lacks both a beginning and an end; it opens with Judas' agreement to betray Christ and concludes with a musically notated vernacular *planctus* that is to be sung by the Virgin. Recently, David Bevington has suggested the play may have begun with Christ's entry into Jerusalem and ended with his appearance to the apostles after the Resurrection.[2] Even as a fragment, the Montecassino play is rich in its implications for dramatic history. It places the origin of the medieval Passion drama in Italy rather than Germany where two plays in the *Carmina Burana* date from the thirteenth century. The work shares some sixty lines with a fourteenth-century fragment from Sulmona entitled *Officium quarti militis* and indicates an extensive dramatic work composed at Montecassino after

1. Dom Mauro Inguanez, "Un dramma della Passione del secolo XII," in *Miscellanea Cassinese*, no. 12 (1936). Unless indicated otherwise, all translations of primary and secondary materials are mine.
2. David Bevington, *Medieval Drama* (Boston: Houghton Mifflin, 1975), p. 202.

the abbey's era of prominence under Abbot Desiderius in the late eleventh century.[3]

The most important historical facet of the Montecassino play is that it provides a vantage point on the creation of a new dramatic form in the Middle Ages. The play modifies the view that the Passion drama evolved from the *planctus* or lyric lament in the same way many scholars hold that the Easter and Christmas plays evolved from tropes for those feasts. Inguanez notes that "the *Planctus ante nescia* for example had its origin in the twelfth century. Having now a text of the drama, earlier than or at least contemporary with the *Planctus*, this comes to lose its importance as a creative element for the drama. It becomes simply one of the elements in the formation of the Passion drama and of less importance than another element, the narration of the Passion according to the gospels in the evocative singing of them during the days of Holy Week, even if the singing were not executed in the present dramatic form."[4] One consequence of Inguanez's observation is to redefine the issues of dramatic history and to align them with problems of literary criticism. One must look for the aesthetic rationale behind the Passion drama rather than trace its development from a liturgical form to a dramatic genre.

Francesco Neri asserts that the *planctus* may be even later than the Latin text of the play. In a review of Inguanez's edition, he says, "The examination of the facsimile (quite clear) persuades me that the hands are different: the Latin text is in Beneventan script; the verses in the vernacular present a

---

3. The text of the Sulmona fragment is in Karl Young, *The Drama of the Medieval Church* (Oxford: Clarendon Press, 1933), I, 701–8. The Sulmona piece is preserved on the back of two notarial documents. In his notes, Inguanez points out the correspondences between the two plays.
4. Inguanez, "Un dramma della Passione del secolo XII," p. 18.

formed Gothic which I do not hesitate to assign to the thirteenth century."[5] An anonymous notice in *Studi Romanzi*
similarly concludes the verses were added later.[6] C. S. Gutkind restates the view and finds "the importance of the new
text lies in the fact that it proves that the drama already existed in Italy in the twelfth century, thus radically modifying
the opinion of De Bartholomaeis and Young as to the introduction of the drama into Abruzzi: it must have passed to
Sulmona from Montecassino."[7] Among the early reviewers,
Paolo Toschi departs from these appreciations of the Passion
drama. While recognizing the play's historical importance,
Toschi stresses its artistic achievement. "The narrative," he
says, "is flowing and made vivid here and there by picturesque
touches; the division of the scenes, even in its fidelity to the
borrowed forms, is wisely made; the entire composition reveals in its author no small literary and dramatic quality."[8]
He further contends that the play's scenography refutes the
view that the staging techniques of the early church-drama
have only symbolic meanings.

Inguanez published a revised edition of the Montecassino
text in 1939. Prefaced by Giulio Bertoni's remarks, the edition offers additional paleographical and textual information,
and Inguanez ventures more ample readings for the difficult
passages on the damaged pages of the manuscript. He also
restates his position that the *planctus* and the text were written
in the same hand. The reasons he gives for his view are that
"first of all, the words of the *Planctus* follow immediately

5. Francesco Neri, "Bolletino Bibliografico," *Giornale storico della lettera-tura italiana* 109 (1937), 129–30.
6. "Notizie," *Studi Romanzi* 27 (1937), 147–48.
7. C. S. Gutkind, "Italian Literature to the Renaissance," *Year's Work in Modern Language Studies* 8 (1937), 14.
8. Paolo Toschi, "Bibliografia," *Archivum Romanicum* 21 (1937), 398.

the directions or rubrics which refer to the Virgin's lament. . . . Moreover, they are not written over an erasure, a fact that would demonstrate a later addition; the ink does not differ from that used for the Latin text; and two typical initial letters, N and Q, are identical to those which we find in other parts of the text."[9] A notice in *Studi Romanzi* recorded these changes.[10] Yet until recently the Passion play received attention only in notes to more general studies of the drama.[11]

The play's inclusion at one point in a thirteenth-century monastic register conveys something of the special nature of this work. Most early medieval plays are found in liturgical books, but the Montecassino drama belongs to a different kind of writing. Like other records of the abbey, the play offers itself as a document, in this case about the Passion. The action is set within attempts to make contracts, and it consists of a number of scenes whose staging is sequential or simultaneous. At the beginning Judas approaches Caiaphas to negotiate an exchange with the priests, and at the end the Virgin seeks another kind of agreement in asking Christ, "Remember me in your kingdom." The linguistic structures that underlie the documentary style consistently mix levels of diction. Judas' greeting of Caiaphas leads to an invective against

9. Dom Mauro Inguanez, "Un dramma della Passione del secolo XII," in *Miscellanea Cassinese*, no. 18 (1939), p. 19. All citations of the text of the play will refer to this revised edition.

10. "Notizie. Teatro medievale," *Studi Romanzi* 29 (1942), 139–40.

11. Mary H. Marshall, "Aesthetic Values of the Liturgical Drama," in *English Institute Essays, 1950* (New York: Columbia University Press, 1951), pp. 89–115; rpt. in *Medieval English Drama: Essays Critical and Contextual*, eds. Jerome Taylor and Alan H. Nelson, Patterns in Literary Criticism, 11 (Chicago: The University of Chicago Press, 1972), pp. 28–43; Richard B. Donovan, "Two Celebrated Centers of Medieval Liturgical Drama: Fleury and Ripoll," in *The Medieval Drama and Its Claudelian Revival*, eds. E. Catherine Dunn, Tatiana Fotitch, and Bernard M. Peebles (Washington: Catholic University of America Press, 1970), p. 50; Rosemary Woolf, *The English Mystery Plays* (Berkeley: University of California Press, 1972), pp. 43, 265, 355n.

Christ that characterizes him as a usurper who deceives the people. The term Judas uses for him, *supplantator*, is the one applied to Jacob by ecclesiastical writers when they discuss his taking over Esau's birthright.[12] Judas' iteration of *fraudis* and *fraudulento* in the speech repeats a term (*fraus*, 'deceiver') conventionally used for the devil.

The opening scene thus hinges on matters of 'law' and its transgressions. Judas says he will hand the 'outlaw' Christ over to the priests if they will respond in a way appropriate to his work. The word he uses for the betrayal, *meritis*, normally carries the ecclesiastical sense of 'good works.' Caiaphas promises him thirty coins of full weight, if he does what they want. The priest then gives him the coins, but Judas carries the agreement further by asking for armed men. Caiaphas instructs the men to go with Judas and completes the transaction by telling Judas to lead the men as comrades (*socios*). The men leave immediately for the place where Christ is praying, and they hold council. Judas gives them the signal there for betraying Christ with a kiss.

In the next scene, Judas reverses his earlier invective and echoes Caiaphas' motif of measurement with the term *scrupulum*. He greets Christ as the "teacher of truth in whom no one finds the smallest measure of deceit." Christ, like Caiaphas, asks Judas why he has come and why the men armed with weapons, clubs, and lanterns accompany him. The men cry out against Christ who asks them to let the disciples leave. They seize and bind him at the same time that the disciples flee and Peter slices off Malchus' ear. Christ rebukes Peter

---

12. Egidio Forcellini, *Lexicon Totius Latinitatis*, rev. F. Corradini and J. Perin (1864–1887) (Padua: Gregoriana, 1951), s.v. *supplantator* cites the word in the letters of St. Ambrose and St. Jerome. C. Du Cange, *Glossarium ad Scriptores mediae et infimae Latinitatis* (1678; rpt. Niort: L. Favre, 1883–1887), s.v. *supplantator* cites a legalistic use of the word.

for the attack and reminds him that they are fulfilling the testimony of the prophets. The soldiers then announce they are leading Christ to Caiaphas' house where the scribes and elders hold council. Christ's reminder to Peter of the need for testimony adumbrates the play's emphasis on legal procedure in the scenes that follow the seizure. As Christ stands bound before the council, two men offer testimony about Christ's prediction that the temple will be destroyed and rebuilt after three days. Caiaphas angrily asks whether the testimony is true, but Christ answers only that the priest will see the son of God sitting on the right side of power. Caiaphas rises from his chair and rips his garment, saying, "He blasphemed. Why are we silent? Why do we bother with witnesses?" The men beat Christ and spit on him, while they taunt him, "Prophesy to us now, Christ; tell us who just hit you."

To balance the accusations of the false witnesses and to focus the issue of testimony even more, the play offers a scene that is simultaneous with the arraignment before Caiaphas. The maid at Caiaphas' house asks Peter whether he had been with Christ. He replies by asking her why she is weaving a lie. The woman repeats the question and Peter, taking God as his witness, says he does not know what she is talking about. She comes a third time to ask the question, but Peter swears again that he does not know. At this point the cock crows, and Christ looks over at Peter. Peter leaves weeping and joins the disciples in hiding. There he admits his guilt in lying and uses the legalistic sense of *renuere*, 'to deny a charge,' to say: "My tongue denied him whom I had promised to love." As Peter laments, two other scenes occur. Christ is led bound from Caiaphas' house to Pilate. Meanwhile, Judas returns and throws the coins on a table before Caiaphas. Like Peter, he admits his guilt in "betraying righteous blood." Caiaphas, however, refuses to admit a crime has occurred and insists only that the contract has been fulfilled. "You will get nothing else now," he tells Judas, "We have the man now." Annas resorts to the other basis of medieval law, customary law, in saying that the blood money cannot return to the temple's treasury but that it should be used to buy the field to bury foreigners. Judas goes out to hang himself as the soldiers arrive with Christ at Pilate's house.

When Pilate asks the soldiers why they have brought Christ to him, they present Christ in phrases that recall Judas' invective at the beginning of the play. They convey the priests' request that Christ be crucified for challenging Caesar. Pilate then asks Christ whether he is the king of the Jews, and he observes that many voices accuse him. Christ's answer to Pilate is as indirect as the earlier response to Caiaphas' question. He says simply that he will not contradict what Pilate has said. The priests and soldiers cry out and demand that Christ be put to death. Pilate remarks again that many people testify against him. Christ makes no reply but is taken out, bound to a column, and scourged. As an alternative to the false testimony of the witnesses, the play offers another version of prophecy in the simultaneous scene with Pilate's wife. The scene occurs in the middle of the trial and so asserts the value of prophetic testimony over legal witnessing. As Christ stands bound, a devil appears to Procula in a dream. She immediately calls her maid and tells her to warn Pilate not to trouble the "just man" and "magnificent prophet." The maid goes to Pilate and explains the dream to him, emphasizing the "many visions, apparitions, and horrible dreams." Pilate assures her he will not allow the shedding of blood. The maid returns to Pilate's wife and conveys the assurance to Procula.

She raises her hands to heaven in praise of God's name and then tells the maid to return to the other women who are weaving.

The trial resumes when Christ is brought back into the court. Pilate expresses wonder at Christ's refusal to respond to the accusations, and he asserts his power of freeing Christ or killing him. However, Christ replies that the judge's power is not his own; it is "bestowed on you from above and given from heaven." Pilate's anger then takes over; he rises from his seat and asks the priests and soldiers whether they want Barabbas or "Jesus, condemned by many witnesses." The soldiers call for the crucifixion and the setting free of Barabbas. The priests remind Pilate that Christ has set himself against Caesar. Pilate asks for their advice, but they raise their hands against Christ and demand the crucifixion. Pilate then washes his hands, saying, "Let his blood not touch me." The priests say that his blood is on them and their successors. With this assumption of responsibility, Pilate formally turns Christ over and sets Barabbas free. He underscores their choice by adding, "Do as you will."

After the trial scenes, the play depicts a stylized mocking. The priests and soldiers lead Christ to another place where they begin to spit on his garments. Placing a reed in his hand, they spit in his face and beat him on the head. Then they dress him in purple and put a crown of thorns on his head. As they kneel before Christ, the priests and soldiers say, "Hail now, king of the Jews. Hail, glory of the angels, holding a reed in your right hand." Immediately after the mocking, they carry out Pilate's earlier injunction to "Do as you will" and decide to crucify him. The soldiers remove the purple cloak, put on the other garment, and lead Christ to the hill. They prepare the cross as Christ kneels, raises his hands, and prays for the crucifiers. He is nailed on his cross and it is raised between those of the two thieves, while the other soldiers divide Christ's garment. The remaining portion of the scene develops these images into different kinds of testimony. Caiaphas approaches and ridicules Christ as the one who was going to destroy the temple and rebuild it in three days. Now, he says, let him escape from the cross. As the priest retires and tears his garment, one of the thieves continues his argument, saying that Christ should be able to save himself. The other thief readily acknowledges the justice of the sentence against them (*recto iure*) but distinguishes this justice from that which applies the same sentence (*atro iudicio*, 'black judgment') to the true God. He asks Christ to remember him "when you shall come to the kingdom of God where you rule forever." Christ promises him that he will be in paradise that day. The Virgin, standing with the other women and John, gestures toward her womb and begins weeping. Her vernacular lament ends the play.

Although the language of the play is predominantly Biblical, the action and documentary style turn on the processes and consequences of law. Judas' betrayal takes place under a contractural agreement, and the priests who negotiate with him later appear as judges who rely on both written and customary law. The trial scenes present an action under the conditions of Roman law that remained in force throughout southern Italy from late Antiquity through the Middle Ages. At Montecassino, the writing of the Passion play is roughly contemporary with the transcription of legal works and the teaching of *ars dictaminis* for drafting legal documents.[13] Leo Marsicanus' *Chronicon* of Montecassino ascribes the tran-

13. Charles Homer Haskins, *The Renaissance of the Twelfth Century* (1927; rpt. New York: Meridian Books, 1966), pp. 139–42.

scription of Justinian's *Instituta* and *Novella* to the abbacy of Desiderius.[14] The first nine books of Justinian's *Codex* were transcribed in the twelfth century, and the Decretals of Gratian were copied there around 1146.[15] Caiaphas' mention that the coins for Judas will be of full weight is connected to the insistence of Roman law on precision in legal matters and descriptions. One can see that Judas' betrayal and Peter's denial consequently involve two means of legal exchange. Judas exchanges Christ for money, but Peter's three denials negate his special relation to Christ. The various trial scenes raise the further issue of valid testimony in the legal process. The law usually decided its cases on testimony that it regarded both qualitatively and quantitatively. The witness of certain respected persons weighed more heavily than the testimony of common people. In cases where the witnesses were of equal stature, the number of witnesses decided the matter.

The Passion play treats these concepts of testimony as a major theme. The witnesses who recount Christ's prediction of the destruction of the temple offer a quantitative testimony, and their willingness to testify is set off by Peter's failure to answer the maid's questions truthfully. Pilate also recurs to quantitative testimony when he stipulates the large number of people who bear witness against Christ. However, the second thief's rebuke to this fellow points to a discrepancy in the legal process and opposes the quantitative testimony of the priests and soldiers to a qualitative testimony based on prophecy. When Christ chides Peter for slicing off Malchus' ear, he characterizes the Passion as testimony to the prophecy of redemption. Even though Procula's dream is caused by the

14. Leo Marsicanus, *Chronicon Casinense*, III. 63, in *Patrologia Latina*, ed. J.-P. Migne (Paris, 1895), CLXXIII, 800.

15. *Codicum Casinensium Manuscriptorum Catalogus*, ed. Dom Mauro Inguanez (Montecassino: Badia, 1915), I, pt. 1, nos. 49, 64.

appearance of the devil, it, too, comes as a revelation and represents a type of pagan prophecy. Her sending the maid to Pilate is an attempt to reinstate qualitative testimony in the judicial process. The professions of faith by the second thief and the Virgin offer additional witness to the prophecy at the end of the play.

The incorporation of legal language and judicial process is part of a strategy for defining the Passion play as a distinct genre. In one respect, the playwright wants to emphasize the difference between his work and the traditions of earlier religious dramaturgy. In another, he wants to indicate the aesthetic and literary aims of the play. By choosing the format of a trial, he connects the work to the conventions of early Christian narrative "tragedy." In particular, he aligns the dramatic treatment of the Passion with Prudentius' fourth-century tragedy of the martyr Romanus (*Peristephanon*, X) and Dracontius' retelling of Aeschylus' *Oresteia* in the fifth century. Prudentius' poems on the crowns of martyrdom (*Peristephanon*) and the hours of the day (*Cathemerinon*) are contained in a ninth-century manuscript from Montecassino (Ms. 374). The first work that appears in this manuscript is the poem on Romanus, and the last work is an adaptation of the classical mime to celebrate the feast of Sts. Peter and Paul (*Peristephanon*, XII).[16]

The greater part of the poem on Romanus shows the martyr's trial before a Roman magistrate. The poem ends with mention of an angel's transcription of the trial that survives when the actual court record is lost. Charles Witke attaches a special significance to this concern with writing and documentation. "It should be noted that it is the official (but per-

16. See *Prudence*, ed. M. Lavarenne, 2nd ed. (Paris: Société d'Édition "Les Belles Lettres," 1955), I, xxix.

ishable) written record that the heavenly counterpart amplifies and consecrates. Prudentius, again characteristically, uses
the known and familiar to get at and to present the unseen.
The commonplace *gesta* of the emperor becomes the *liber*
which the eternal judge in heaven reads. The past facts become the ground for future action, and the transitory becomes
the immutable."[17] As we shall see, this connection between
the historical and the transcendent becomes the aesthetic basis
for the Passion play. In Dracontius' *Orestis tragoedia*, the
emphasis on writing and documentation is not so apparent.
However, the poem uses the trial to resolve the issues around
Orestes' vengeance against Clytemnestra and later Pyrrhus.
In a way that anticipates Christ's rebuke to Pilate in the Montecassino play, it sets divine power above the court by having
Minerva intervene to cast the decisive vote for Orestes'
acquittal.

The Passion drama moves still further toward defining its
own genre by reshaping the Biblical narrative in a new structure. Unlike the *Ludus breuiter de passione* from the *Carmina
Burana*, the Montecassino text combines the Scriptural passages into a work that is different from its sources. The legal
borrowings provide some measure of the difference, but the
addition of apocryphal and classical sources underscores the
literary nature of the work. The play relies primarily on
Matthew's gospel with supplementing passages from John
and Luke. However, for Procula's dream it goes to the apocryphal *Acta Pilati* which is the only source to record the details. The playwright's stylistic model marks an even greater
divergence from a purely Scriptural drama. Caiaphas' descrip-

17. Charles Witke, *Numen Litterarum. The Old and the New in Latin
Poetry from Constantine to Gregory the Great*, Mittellateinische Studien und
Texte, V (Leiden: E. J. Brill, 1971), p. 141.

tion of Judas as "seeking our doorway" (*nostra petens limina* —v. 6) is a reminiscence of the passage in the *Aeneid* (II. 256) where the Greek fleet stealthily approaches the Trojan shore from Tenedos (*litora nota petens*). The model for the scene with Procula is also in Virgil. The "visions, apparitions, and horrible dreams" that the maid reports to Pilate recall Dido's terrifying dreams about the old prophecies (*Aeneid*, IV. 460–73). This same passage in the *Aeneid* refers to drama in mentioning "Orestes, the son of Agamemnon, driven wildly on stage" (*Agamemnonius scaenis agitatus Orestes*). Even Procula's initial order to the maid, "Stop the delays and hurry" (*Tolle moras et festina*), may derive from the scene in which the image of Mercury appears to the sleeping Aeneas and tells him, "Up and get to it. Break up the delays" (*Heia age, rumpe moras*) [IV. 596].

WESTERN LITURGICAL DRAMA

In creating a new form, the Passion play consciously diverges from the liturgical drama that has been seen as the origin of most Western medieval drama. Nevertheless, it will be useful to examine this liturgical drama as a way of determining the special nature of the Passion play. The removal of the *quem queritis* trope from the Introit of the Easter Mass and its placement in the Easter Matins office gave rise to an action in which the Marys approach the tomb to anoint the body of Christ and exchange dialogue with an angel who tells them of the Resurrection. Karl Young points out the artistic limitations of the early forms. He says that in this first stage of the *Visitatio Sepulchri*, "the chief interest . . . arises not so much from the dramatic utterances themselves as from the accompanying rubrics. The speeches . . . are in large measure formalized, and lack variety, whereas the stage-directions frequently disclose fresh details as to the manner in which the words are spoken, as to the physical setting, and, most important of all, as to the impersonating of the characters." Later stages of the *Visitatio* include the apostles Peter and Paul and introduce the risen Christ into the action; at times a scene is added for the spice merchant. The liturgical context of the works is established in the rubrics which typically prescribe that the *Te Deum laudamus* be sung at the completion of the play. The development of the pieces has largely to do with amplification. Young notes that "most of the utterances added to the original dialogue of the *Quem quaeritis*, to be sure, are passages from the authorized liturgy, adopted into the play with very little effort towards readjustment."[18] In later stages of the *Visitatio*, the sequence *Victimae paschali* is a common addition. The changes made in the texts indicate the emphasis is on elaborating the original trope, yet the trope, as Oscar Cargill maintained long ago, is a lyric piece rather than a dramatic form.[19]

The music accompanying the liturgical plays is in the style of Gregorian chant in the early manuscripts, and its effect is to highlight the action. William L. Smoldon observes that "the more dramatic moments were usually reserved for solo voices and were in swift-moving recitative: but impressive choral climaxes were not lacking. This art flourished throughout the Middle Ages and must have established a strong tradition of performance." In many cases the music is a free composition, and this quality affords the playwright flexibility in depicting his characters. Several later pieces show changes in dramatic emotions as one character takes over the tune of an-

18. Young, *The Drama of the Medieval Church*, I, 239–40, 272.

19. Oscar Cargill, *Drama and Liturgy* (New York: Columbia University Press, 1930).

other. The transference also occurs between the music of different kinds of liturgical plays. Smoldon notes, for example, that the thirteenth-century *Officium Pastorum* from Rouen represents such a mixture. "The scene at the crib when the midwives draw aside the curtains consists mainly of the trope dialogue with its usual music. There is one modification: the setting of the first four words of the midwives' question is not the usual Christmas tune, but the notes of 'Quem quaeritis in sepulchro?' The spell of the older melody prevails for this brief time, and then the usual setting is resumed."[20] This kind of musical sophistication channels embellishment toward the evocation of mystery. As Clifford Davidson argues, "the composers and singers of the music of the Christian liturgy turned their incantations to the task of setting forth affecting and powerful images representing the various events of the Christian story. The writers, producers, and actors of the liturgical drama were pursuing similar aims. The music and images are intended to take us back to the sepulchre and to the manger where the Incarnation signalled a new beginning for history."[21]

The *Regularis Concordia* of St. Ethelwold, written in 965–75 for the Benedictines in England, represents the event of man's redemption in a form that unites dramatic action and the ritual celebration of Christian mystery. This *Visitatio* combines several modes of choral address, and its rubrics displace action from a naturalistic plane by calling for liturgical vestments and staging the piece in the area of the altar. While the third lesson of Matins is being sung, four of the monks

20. William L. Smoldon, "Liturgical Drama," in *New Oxford History of Music*, ed. Dom Anselm Hughes (London: Oxford University Press, 1954), II, 175, 197.

21. Clifford Davidson, "Medieval Drama: Diversity and Theatricality," *Comparative Drama* 8 (1974), 8–9.

vest themselves. One wears an alb and carries a palm in his hand. He approaches the liturgical sepulchre and quietly seats himself. The others, vested in copes and carrying censers, move as if searching for something and finally come to the sepulchre. "These things are done," the text explains, "in imitation of the angel sitting in the tomb and the women coming with spices so that they might anoint the body of Jesus."[22] The angel sees them approach and asks in a voice of medium pitch, "Whom do you seek in the sepulchre, O followers of Christ?" The three women reply in unison, "Jesus of Nazareth crucified, O heavenly one." The angel tells them, "He is not here; he arose just as he predicted. Go, announce that he has risen from the dead." The women carry out the command and in so doing blur the distinction between self-contained dramatic representation and ritual participation. By turning toward the choir and singing, "Alleluia, the Lord has risen; the strong lion has risen this day, Christ, the son of God," they reshape the limits of time and make the congregation a witness to the unique events of Christian history.

The angel continues this expansion beyond naturalistic representation. He seats himself and, as if calling the women back, sings the antiphon, "Come and see the place where the Lord was laid. Alleluia." He then rises and lifts the veil of the sepulchre to show them the cloths in which the cross has been wrapped. The women put down the censers which they had brought with them into the sepulchre and display the cloth to the clergy. The rubrics which describe this action stress again the congregation's presence at the event. The women display the cloth to show "that the Lord arose and was not now wrapped in it." They sing the antiphon, "The

22. Text in Young, *The Drama of the Medieval Church*, I, 249–50.

Lord who hung for us on the cross has risen from the sepulchre. Alleluia," and place the cloth on the altar. The prior, rejoicing with them, begins the *Te Deum laudamus* as all the bells ring. The scenario preserved in the *Regularis Concordia* thus moves along principles of reversal and expansion. The Marys' initial action "in imitation of looking for something" resolves itself in their placing the cloth on a liturgical altar. Their shared sorrow is transformed into a communal celebration with the final hymn.

This affective return to origins connects the liturgical plays to ritual structures rather than the form of the drama. In contradistinction to drama whose aim and effects are social, ritual intends to remove the participants from ordinary existence and situate them in a realm of sanctified time and cultic mystery. The circumscribed world of art may be different from nature but it does not promise the deliverance of religion. C. Clifford Flanigan finds that the exchanges of dialogue in these *quem queritis* tropes "do not represent a unique seeking after dramatic modes within the liturgy. Rather, they operate according to a cultic notion of imitation which makes the past event a present reality." The *quem queritis* trope "reveals in an extraordinarily clear manner the whole conceptual basis of the Christian liturgy. It is not merely that the past event of salvation is made present again; the worshipping community of the tenth century is thought here to become identical with the Marys of the first century. Both seek the crucified Lord, both hear the angelic reply that he is risen, both are confronted with the actual presence of the resurrected Lord himself, both respond with a joyous song of praise."[23]

23. C. Clifford Flanigan, "The Liturgical Context of the *Quem Queritis* Trope," *Comparative Drama* 8 (1974), 55.

Montecassino had its own *quem queritis* trope, dating from the end of the eleventh century, and the Passion dramatist signals the difference between his work and the liturgical form by including the trope in his play.[24] Christ ends his address to Judas and the armed men with the command, "Dicite quem queritis" ("tell me whom you seek"—v. 45). From this reference to the liturgical drama, one must presume that the later creation of a Passion play constitutes a response to the differences that are apparent in the two forms. Whereas the liturgical pieces rely on a structure of sympathy, the Passion drama attempts to portray empathetically events that are unique and transcendent. This intention allows the dramatist to create a new work from other literary materials and to replace the amplification of the liturgical plays with rhetorical principles. In the Montecassino text, these principles develop from the process of law and testimony and give the Gospel accounts an aesthetic shape. Behind that shape is an element of distance which liturgy and liturgical drama do not accept. Unlike the Marys at the sepulchre, the false witnesses of the Passion drama are unable to address an audience directly and to bring it within the circuit of action. Instead, their moral choices can only image those of the audience. Thus the nature of imitation remains different from liturgical enactment. The play does not originate in the action of mystery; it originates in the intention to translate mystery into other structures.

EASTERN LITURGICAL DRAMA

The qualities that distinguish the Passion play from the liturgical drama of the Western church also distinguish it from the dramatic liturgical forms in the Eastern rite. Monte-

24. Dom Mauro Inguanez, "Il 'Quem quaeritis' pasquale nei Codici Cassinesi," *Studi medioevali* 14 (1941), 142–49.

cassino had close relations with the East during the abbacy of Desiderius (1058–1086), and these ties might suggest the influence of works like the kontakia. The kontakia are versified sermons whose stanzas have identical meters and end in the same refrain. They are accompanied by a prelude in a different meter. The use of dialogues and monologues gives these homilies a dramatic character. The kontakion itself seems to have developed from earlier forms in the Syriac church. Marjorie Carpenter states that, "clearly, the Syrian hymns and homilies are related to the Greek homilies, for the same type of biblical allusion and the same sort of references to the Gospels appear in both. Some similarities would necessarily occur, since the purpose of each form was to follow the readings in the liturgy. The method of expanding the stories so that they become dramatic and are clothed in rhythmic phrases is, however, a characteristic that supports a theory of common origin for both Greek and Syrian expressions."[25]

Giorgio La Piana finds a dramatic cycle deriving from the homilies in the pre-Iconoclastic age. At first the homilies "contain dialogues, sometimes of considerable length, which are merely paraphrases of short dialogues of the canonical texts." Later, the dialogues and monologues are "altogether new creations, even when connected, as almost in each case, with a sacred text." Finally, the homilies become dramatized episodes about Christ and the Virgin. La Piana maintains that in this last group "the dramatic scenes were originally independent of the oratorical parts and that the homilies, as we have them now, are arbitrary later arrangements of passages from preëxisting dramatic compositions and in some

25. Marjorie Carpenter, *Kontakia of Romanos, Byzantine Melodist* (Columbia, Missouri: University of Missouri Press, 1970), I, xix.

cases from old sermons."[26] These works develop their own
rhythmic systems, but their basis remains in the oratory popu-
larized by the great preachers among the early Greek Fathers.

The most famous writer of kontakia is the sixth-century
Byzantine melodist Romanos. His kontakia on the Passion
themes present a vivid account of the event but emphasize
again the need to distinguish the dramatic from drama. They
have a dramatic interchange among voices elaborated as the
circumstances require but without a sense of dramatic space.
Their interchanges develop from various discrepancies. Judas
strikes a bargain with Caiaphas although he "carried complete
wealth." The kontakion for Holy Thursday attributes the
bargain to his character: "Now your insatiate nature has appeared; now has been made clear that you will never be satis-
fied. / O, ravenous, dissolute, implacable, / Shameless, and
gluttonous, foolish and avaricious." Mary's dialogue with
Christ reflects the differing human and divine perspectives
on his sacrifice. The kontakion on the Passion centers on the
discrepancies among kinds of law. In leading Christ to the
court of Caiaphas and charging that he has defied the law of
Moses, the "lawless" people demonstrate the kind of strict
legalism for which the devil will compliment them in another kontakion. At the court Caiaphas is described as jealous,
and Cain's envy of Abel becomes a precedent for what Christ
is going to endure. The crowd demands crucifixion but Christ
is handed over to Pilate in a further distortion of justice:
"They handed over to the court of justice the One who will
judge kings and peasants; / The condemned judges the last

26. Giorgio La Piana, "The Byzantine Theater," *Speculum* 11 (1936),
176–77; La Piana examines the problem in detail in *Le Rappresentazioni sacre
nella letteratura Bizantina dalle Origini al Secolo IX, con Rapporti al Teatro
Sacro d'Occidente* (Grottaferata: Tipografia Italo-Orientale S. Nilo, 1912).

Judge; / The one who lives unknown threatened to kill like a thief the Redeemer." Christ refuses to answer the charges Pilate announces, but he tells the people "Death is a debt I owed." The crowd replies that Christ will die "as one breaking the Sabbath," yet he asserts his power to supersede the law with miracles. Pilate's wife adds testimony to this power when she tells her husband, "You are judging your judge." By washing his hands, Pilate thinks "He would be held guiltless; but he was found to be responsible."[27]

The kontakia differ from the liturgical drama of the West by the intrusion of narrative. The sung voices of the characters alternate not just with each other in dialogue but also with a level of commentary and exposition that the Western plays typically confine to the rubrics. The intrusion of such commentary owes in large part to the kontakia's nature as a dramatized homily, but it also shows a different concept of amplification. Whereas the liturgical plays expand dramatic action, the kontakia amplify emotions. In Mary's kontakion at the cross, "the dramatic or mimetic action is not simply an adjunct to the liturgical action but rather constitutes an expansion of it by eliminating any restraint placed upon the Virgin's self-assertion by the strictly liturgical phase of the drama being memorated."[28] Placed within a framework of commentary and exposition, these expansions lead to a choral affirmation whose basis is an understanding of the emotions. The expansions in the Western plays substitute for this understanding the inclusion of its participants in a broader cultic action.

Although the kontakia assume dramatic features, they do

27. The translations are by Carpenter, *Kontakia of Romanos*, I, 174–75, 209, 210, 212.
28. Sandro Sticca, "The *Christos Paschon* and the Byzantine Theater," *Comparative Drama* 8 (1974), 20.

not constitute drama. Sandro Sticca maintains, "they have a potentiality for performance but clearly lack the essentials of the theater, which requires scenic actions actually performed by actors impersonating the characters with voice and gestures."[29] The interchange of voices belongs more to a choral structure than to the impersonation insisted on by Young and E. K. Chambers, and the gestures are those of declamation and not imitation.[30] The expositions that accompany the interchanges further remove the kontakia from drama as a form. The Montecassino playwright relies on expository techniques to identify his scenes to the audience and give his play an iconic style, but the melodist goes on to expose the meaning of his scenes. As a result, his work is unable to image the events of Christian history. The intent of its paraphrastic commentary is to displace action into a series of multiple statements whose cumulative effect is an emotional reinforcement. The responses of the auditors are orchestrated by the liturgical piece, and the element of moral choice posited by Christian drama becomes illusory. The rhetorical principles of the Passion drama allow its writer to sketch examples of choice at a distance, but the choral structure of the dramatic homilies permits one only to affirm choices made in history.

The only genuine dramatic work of the early Byzantine theater is the *Christos Paschon*, which is dated variously from the fourth to the eleventh centuries. Sticca connects it to Gregory Nazianzenus and the fifth century. The drama is a composite of 2602 lines based on a number of plays by Euripides and so differs from works based upon Biblical sources. The play uses the chorus of classical Greek tragedy to relate

29. Ibid., p. 20.
30. Young, *The Drama of the Medieval Church*, I, 80; E. K. Chambers, *The Mediaeval Stage* (Oxford: Clarendon Press, 1903), I, 81.

Christ's Passion and death, his entombment, and the Resurrection. The dynamic of the play, as the prologue announces, is between divinity and humanity, and the problems of testimony are subsumed by these larger issues. Sticca observes that "Gregory lends the greatest effectiveness to the theological dimension of Christ's Incarnation and Passion by the most intense expression of 'human' experience: by making Mary the central figure of the play and by defining and revealing the full intensity of her suffering."[31] He proposes that in performance the "movements and gestures of grief, pain, and joy" would resemble those depicted by illustrations of the Passion, and he suggests that areas of the basilica may have been used to stage the drama.

THE CENTO

Against the background of liturgical drama in the East and West, a work like the Montecassino Passion assumes a special character. It diverges from the liturgical forms by separating its action from the cultic and didactic functions, and it approaches other techniques of composition that were popular in late Antiquity and the Middle Ages. The most common of these techniques is the practice of the cento or composing new works out of pieces of earlier texts. Virgil was the most frequent source for the new works. Domenico Comparetti observes that "by the adroit combination of isolated lines and hemistichs, Vergil was made to say the most unexpected things." Christians used the form to have him testify to their faith. Proba Faltonia composed the Old Testament story in Virgilian verses; Pomponius created a similar work to honor Christ. In the fourth century, Marcus Victorinus made a hymn on the Passion, and in the fifth century Sedulius

31. Sticca, "The *Christos Paschon* and the Byzantine Theater," p. 29.

fashioned a poem on the Incarnation. The practice became so widespread among Christians that in a Decretal of 494, Pope Gelasius had to declare the works apocryphal.[32] At Montecassino, a similar approach to composition appears in the subscriptions to manuscripts, where the scribes add their own verses to the materials they have copied out. Francis Newton remarks that such compositions are often made up of taglines and common expressions. They have the appearance of being original works, when in reality they offer little more than new arrangements of general formulas.[33]

In following the centoist's approach to composition, the Montecassino playwright duplicates the process of writing what may be the first medieval play. David N. Dumville finds a Harrowing of Hell play in the English Book of Cerne which he dates to the first half of the eighth century, some two centuries before the liturgical *quem queritis* of the *Visitatio*. The piece begins with the rubric, "This is the speech of the innumerable holy people who were held in the captivity of hell." Their speech calls for Christ to "save the dead captives of hell" and forgive their sins. Christ comes and frees them from their chains, but Adam and Eve remain bound. Adam supplicates to Christ in a tearful and miserable voice: "Have mercy on me, God, have mercy on me in your great compassion, and in the multitude of your pities wipe out my iniquity because I sinned only to you and committed evil before you." Christ takes pity on him and the chains are broken. Adam then falls in front of the Lord to offer praise for curing "all my feebleness." However, Eve persists in crying and tells Christ that she recognizes the justice of his judgment

32. Domenico Comparetti, *Vergil in the Middle Ages*, trans. E. F. M. Benecke (1895; rpt. London: George Allen & Unwin, 1966), pp. 53-55.

33. Francis Newton, "Beneventan Scribes and Subscriptions With a List of Those Known at the Present Time," *The Bookmark* 43 (1973), 1-35.

"for when I was held in honor, I did not understand." She prays, "Do not turn the face of your mercy from me and do not fall into anger on account of your handmaiden."

At this point the text breaks off, but Dumville speculates, "It seems that the original conclusion of the 'Cerne' piece must have occurred with the chorus of praise by Abraham and all the delivered souls." He observes that the work contains "two sections for each of the performers, each section being supplied with a short narrative introduction. It would end, as it began, with a choral ensemble; but the joyous conclusion would provide for the whole work the progression from sorrow to joy, observed too in each of the three individual scenes."[34] In this mixture of narrative with speeches, the piece is close to the technique of the kontakion. It resembles the Montecassino Passion in the reshaping of earlier literary texts. The Cerne "Harrowing of Hell" depends on a Latin homily which survives only in an Old English version. This text is a combination of a pseudo-Augustinian homily and material about Adam and Eve. The play adds to the composite homily a number of verses from the Roman Psalter. The author's intention to create a new work from the sources is apparent in these redirections of the original narrative.

The late appearance of a play exclusively concerned with the Passion is commonly attributed to the central position of the Mass. Young infers that "the representation of the last occurrences in Christ's life was deliberately avoided" and that "for bringing vividly before the medieval worshipper

34. David N. Dumville, "Liturgical Drama and Panegyric Responsory from the Eighth Century: A Re-examination of the Origin and Contents of the Ninth-Century Section of the Book of Cerne," *Journal of Theological Studies* 23 (1972), 380. I owe my knowledge of this article to a paper by O. B. Hardison, Jr., "Some Questions in the History of Liturgical Drama," read at the University of Toronto February 8, 1974.

the great Immolation, the Mass itself was felt to be sufficiently effective. Since by visible and audible means the celebrant could bring about daily an actual repetition of the great Sacrifice, what need was there of imitating it through the imperfect means of impersonation and stagecraft?"[35] This view not only explains why the Passion play is a relatively late topic for the medieval dramatist; it also explains why the Passion play should never have developed. In the Middle Ages, the Mass never lost its effectiveness in conveying the mystery of the spiritual sacrifice. The very effectiveness would, in fact, create the need to develop an aesthetic form to express the Passion in conditions other than those of mystery. The liturgy abolishes profane space and time and thus locates the major events of the redemption in a transcendent realm. To recover them, one must devise other forms that remain within time and operate under different conventions.

The commentaries on the Mass provide one form for this recovery under the conventions of narrative and analogy, and scholars have pointed to the influence of the commentaries on medieval thinking about the Passion. In the preface to his *Liber officialis* (821–835), Amalarius of Metz reveals that his age has lost an understanding of the reasons behind the order of the Mass now celebrated by custom. As O. B. Hardison, Jr., asserts, Amalarius' work "answered a strongly felt need for an interpretation of the Mass which emphasized its immediate, as against its historical, significance." The basis of the interpretation is a combination of authority and intuition. "In everything I write," Amalarius says, "I depend on the judgment of the holy men and the pious Fathers; nevertheless, I say what I perceive."[36] The most prominent feature

---

35. Young, *The Drama of the Medieval Church*, I, 492.
36. Amalarius of Metz, *Liber officialis*, in *Patrologia Latina*, CV, 988–89.

of his interpretation is a view of the Mass as an allegory in which the participants apprehend mystery as if it were a sacred drama. Hardison comments that "from beginning to end, but especially during the Canon and the Communion, the Mass is a rememorative drama depicting the life, ministry, crucifixion, and resurrection of Christ. Although other elements vary according to the ingenuity of the interpreter, rememorative allegory is always present."[37] This style of allegory and the multiple values of its symbols would, however, give the Mass an episodic structure rather than the single, contained action that classical theorists prefer in the drama. Moreover, the emphasis of rememorative allegory on immediate significance indicates that the dramatic elements have more to do with emotive responses than with aesthetic form.

Honorius of Autun's *Gemma animae* (c. 1100) seems to expand Amalarius' sense of the dramatic into a formal analysis of the Mass as sacred drama. It connects the recitation of tragedy in theaters to the sacrifice of the Mass so that "our *tragicus* represents by his gestures to the Christian people Christ's battle in the theater of the church and teaches them the victory of his redemption." Prayers and gestures symbolize the various episodes of the Passion. The *Orate fratres* expresses Christ's undertaking suffering. The silence of the *Secretum* represents the lamb being led to sacrifice, and the extension of the hands signifies Christ on the cross. Chanting the preface recalls his cries, while the secret prayers of the Canon are like the silence of Holy Saturday. The Kiss of Peace at the end of the Mass stands for the peace after the resurrection. "When the sacrifice is finished," Honorius ex-

---

37. O. B. Hardison, Jr., *Christian Rite and Christian Drama in the Middle Ages: Essays in the Origin and Early History of Modern Drama* (Baltimore: The Johns Hopkins Press, 1965), pp. 38, 44.

plains, "peace and communion are given to the people because, our accuser having been defeated by our warrior in the duel, peace is announced to the people by the judge and they are invited to the feast."[38] With the dismissal, *Ite missa est*, they return to their homes rejoicing. Hardison finds in the passage a developed concept of dramaturgy. "Honorius not only uses the vocabulary of dramatic criticism, he uses it with considerable sophistication. The church is regarded as a theater. The drama enacted has a coherent plot based on conflict (*duellum*) between a champion and an antagonist."[39] The conflict is shaped by a rising action, reversal, and catharsis.

The details of Honorius' description suggest that his analogue for the Mass is something different from a drama conceived along Aristotelian lines. The mention of reciting tragedies would characterize drama as a form of declamation given in a place more akin to a public forum than a stage. The *tragicus* who presents Christ's battles is not a tragic actor or author; he is the orator whose exaggerated gestures in delivery, as Cicero (*De oratore* [LI]) remarks, can inflate the importance of any matter before a court. In this instance, he evokes a scene which interprets man's state as it directly concerns matters of law. Christ and the accuser appear before a judge in a dispute over property and administration. The title applied to Christ, *agonotheta*, originally means the overseer of games in Sparta. In the legal tradition of the *Digesta Justiniana*, the *agonotheta* is an official responsible for administering state and personal property under legal statutes. The controversy thus revolves around possession of mankind, and a court would have to view the issue under its own procedures for

38. Honorius of Autun, *Gemma animae*, in *Patrologia Latina*, CLXXII, 570.

39. Hardison, *Christian Rite and Christian Drama in the Middle Ages*, p. 40.

evidence. Yet in this dispute over mankind after the fall, the issue cannot be resolved by judicial arguments or testimony. The litigants have recourse only to the *duellum* or judicial duel. As an orator, the celebrant would be citing the precedent of this duel for the reenactment seen in the Mass. He would argue Christ's victory demonstrates the primacy of grace and immanent justice over secular legal processes, just as the Montecassino Passion dramatist establishes prophetic testimony over the witnessing in Pilate's court.

The difference between emphasizing the dramatic elements of the Mass and constructing a Passion play reflects a fundamental difference in contexts. Amalarius and Honorius write in the tradition of Gallican cathedral worship, whose features are Oriental and theatrical.[40] They conceive of the Passion as a victory by Christ and devise elaborate patterns of responding to it. For the Montecassino playwright, the context is defined by monastic liturgy, and his age regards the Passion through contemplative forms. The suffering Christ replaces Christ the victor, and the embellished modes of responding to mystery give way to the human realities in Christian history. Sticca asserts that "there can be no doubt that mystical contemplation of the doctrine of the Incarnation must have contributed to arouse the desire to represent the Passion dramatically."[41] The elaborate lyrical responses of the Gallican rite are an aesthetic prelude to the singing of the Passion Gospels which Sticca takes as "the one germ which

40. Léopold Duchesne, *Origines du culte chrétien*, 5th ed. (Paris: Editions E. de Boccard, 1925), pp. 93–99. For recent discussion, see C. Clifford Flanigan, "The Roman Rite and the Origins of the Liturgical Drama," *University of Toronto Quarterly* 43 (1973–74), 263–84.
41. Sandro Sticca, "The Literary Genesis of the Latin Passion Play," in *The Medieval Drama*, ed. Sandro Sticca (Albany: State University of New York Press, 1972), p. 45.

could have been developed in the creation of the first Passion Play."[42]

To the extent that ritual embodies dramatic qualities and the commentators recognize its theatricality, liturgy remains a possible source for the creation of a Passion drama. Yet the composition of a work that focuses on Christ's humanity and expresses transcendent events in temporal structures requires a context that is not exclusively liturgical. Such a context would assimilate a variety of sources and influences. Sticca holds that the Montecassino text is the product of such a mixed environment. It is "inspired by the liturgical services of Good Friday, the Gospel accounts, and particularly by the confluence and coexistence, beginning with the eleventh century, of three themes: in liturgy, a concentration on Christocentric piety; in art, a more humanistic treatment of Christ; in literature, a consideration of the scenes of the Passion as dramatic and human episodes."[43] The impact of these influences is to direct the play away from the impressionism of the commentaries and to examine the Passion in terms set up by other forms. From the combination of sources, the playwright attempts to create a separate imaginative work.

The joining of liturgical, artistic, and literary sources into an independent structure demonstrates the Montecassino play's aim of being an aesthetic form instead of a variation on ritual observance. The writer's choice of a dramatic mode is a conscious decision made possible but not determined by his cultural context. Just as Hrotswitha of Gandersheim adapts the modes of Terence's comedies in the tenth century to pro-

42. Sandro Sticca, "The Priority of the Montecassino Passion Play," *Latomus* 20 (1961), 839.

43. Sandro Sticca, *The Latin Passion Play: Its Origins and Development* (Albany: State University of New York Press, 1970), p. 173.

vide moral instruction for the nuns under her charge, the Montecassino playwright adapts dramatic forms to assert the continuing historicity of the Passion. His theme of law is related to an insistence on moral choice in history. The play functions as a contemporary document about the Passion, and by being a record made in time it is able to move in a different direction from liturgy. Its documentary nature allows the playwright to render the transcendent as if it were contemporary and historical. He can recover the unique, past events, with the illusion of their being able to be duplicated through writing and imagination. In this recovery, the play presents to an audience the action that the Mass symbolizes for its congregation.

The innovations of the Montecassino playwright contrast with the aesthetic choice made a century later by the author of the *Ludus de passione* from Benediktbeuern. Young notes the German play's diversity of action and concludes that "a dramatic piece so loosely and casually arranged may best be regarded not as an attempt towards a closely knit play, but as an episodic religious opera."[44] He maintains its loose structure would lead to expansions that could not be adapted to a liturgical service. However, Michael Rudick argues for the work's place in the Procession of Palms in the Palm Sunday liturgy. The liturgy for Lent and Holy Week is the playwright's major source, and he shapes his material around the themes of redemption and salvation that dominate the liturgy of the season. In consequence, the play offers "a didactically structured plot whose incidents are chosen and arranged as a means of illustrating or enforcing certain tenets of the Christian faith" rather than a plot that follows the

44. Young, *The Drama of the Medieval Church*, I, 536.

chronology of the Gospel accounts. This choice of an episodic framework based on larger liturgical patterns reflects in turn the different objectives of the Montecassino and Benedikt-beuern texts. The Montecassino play attempts "to recreate events in at least a semi-realistic manner in order that they become apprehensible as history to an audience and thus become the grounds for devotion, while the Benediktbeuern play seeks to embody doctrine and does so less through realistic story-telling than through selection of incidents and for the most part stylized representation within a liturgical context."[45]

The difference between these intentions derives from separate understandings of poetics and aesthetics. Both works are the products of monastic circles, but each play proceeds on discrete assumptions about the nature of the drama. In connecting his drama to the Holy Week liturgy, the Benedikt-beuern playwright establishes a connection between representation and reference so that the events made vivid in ritual can be amplified through representation. His poetics is based on a dynamics of imitation in which the audience apprehends the meaning of the work by its proximity and similarity to the Holy Week rituals. The drama is, in short, a conscious modification of ritual. For the Montecassino playwright, the issue of imitation is more complex. His work echoes some tonalities of the Good Friday office but does not rely on that office for verbal borrowings. For him the relation of drama to liturgy points up the differences between the forms. In depicting the Passion sequence, he remains closer to the plasticity of events than to their doctrinal meanings. His place-

45. Michael Rudick, "Theme, Structure, and Sacred Context in the Bene-diktbeuern 'Passion' Play," *Speculum* 49 (1974), 283, 285.

ment of choral action within the drama isolates the audience from the lyricism of communal affirmation and the shared experiences of ritual celebration.

In performance, these aesthetic emphases lead into something different from the naturalistic extravagance of drama in the late Middle Ages. The acting would remain consistent with the play's documentary and legalistic style. As early as Tertullian's *Apologeticus*, addressed to the Roman magistrates of the second century, Christian writers had stressed the forensic qualities of their works, and the Montecassino playwright continues the tradition. In the trial scenes, his characters adopt a rhetorical delivery, and elsewhere their performances show the exaggeration on which Cicero comments. Caiaphas' gesture in ripping his garment seems related to this "tragic" style, and the soldiers' actions in beating Christ are similarly exaggerated. In these two scenes, moreover, one finds the documentary element supported by an expository technique in which the actors label their actions. The technique lends an iconic sense to the action and further refines it by substituting a formalized depiction for an impressionistic or symbolic representation of the Passion. If the play were performed within the basilica itself along the lines of the Byzantine drama, the formalized depiction would go even further to merge with the iconographical programs inside the church and present a highly conscious rhetorical work.

The audience witnessing such a production may have combined laity and the monks of the abbey. The inclusion of the vernacular *planctus* at the end of the play suggests some lay members were in the audience. Yet even in this mixed audience, the dramatist expects social cohesion. The audience does not require a parallel commentary to the Latin text or a stage director to explain the action. The expository techniques appear to be adequate in Latin; and, when the Virgin makes her lament in Italian, the effect is to join the witness of ordinary speech to that of the Biblical language.[46] The audience is unified on still another basis. It would tend to connect the dramatist's experiments in re-creating the Passion through visual images and rhetorical persuasion with contemporary attempts to regain historical and typological aspects of the Christian past. Perhaps more than any other audience for the medieval drama, the Cassinesi of the twelfth century could appreciate the writer's efforts to devise a new form that would recover the shapes of events.

What one has, then, in the twelfth-century Passion play is an aesthetic distancing that modifies both classical and liturgical notions of imitation. Aristotle's view of classical drama stresses its repetition and recurrence. The logic of such representation is syllogistic; it evolves from amassing examples of categories of action and establishing models of predictability. From these models the dramatist can judge which actions are likely in human experience and hence credible in a dramatic form. Amalarius' view that "sacraments should have some appearance of the things for which they are sacraments" defines the major tendency of liturgical imitation.[47] The gestures and objects of ritual symbolize various events of Christian history but do not project them as aesthetic images. The Montecassino Passion diverges from these two traditions by incorporating in its narrative both the unique events of Christ's Passion and the predictable reactions of characters to

46. Woolf, *The English Mystery Plays*, pp. 43–44, observes that the vernacular is often used in laments for purely literary reasons.
47. Amalarius of Metz, *Liber officialis*, in *Patrologia Latina*, CV, 989.

that sacrifice. Whereas classical theater deals primarily with actions that can be repeated in history and nature, the Passion play centers on the singularity of Christ's suffering. This focus demands an orientation different from the kind of symbolism Amalarius prescribes. It also requires a dramatist whose motive is to synthesize the transcendent and historical aspects of his material.

2. The Aesthetics of Recovery

WE ARE accustomed to viewing the medieval drama in terms borrowed from other historical periods. The Middle Ages had no consistent or programmatic attitude toward the drama, and the tendency of modern critics is to align the plays with the conventions of either Aristotle or modern drama. In his introduction to a recent collection of essays on medieval English drama, Jerome Taylor asserts the continuing value of Aristotelian principles. "Material means, dramatic manner, 'action' expressed, effect achieved: such parameters systematize analysis as one measures their changing values. Regulative of critical focus, appropriate to the texts under scrutiny, and productive of definition, they allow applicable discriminations to be discriminately combined."[1] These categories are proper to a developed genre. They assume that the drama has attained a public and conventional character and that it will respond to the expectations of an audience, much as tradition creates a critic's expectations. In early works or consciously innovative pieces, however, these modes of analysis often prove inadequate. Aristotle seems

1. Jerome Taylor, "Critics, Mutations, and Historians of Medieval English Drama," in *Medieval English Drama: Essays Critical and Contextual*, eds. Jerome Taylor and Alan H. Nelson, Patterns in Literary Criticism, 11 (Chicago: The University of Chicago Press, 1972), pp. 11–12.

hopelessly inept in dealing with portions of Aeschylus, and for the medieval drama it is similarly difficult to analyze the early plays from the vantage point of later dramatic conventions. Instead, one has to consider the factors that would go into writing new works and examine their impact on the plays. Such a study is admittedly speculative, but it promises the advantage of seeing the work in a wider aesthetic and cultural perspective.

In the past century, scholars have used a ritual context for understanding the drama that reappears in the West during the Middle Ages. From Marius Sepet's essays beginning in the 1860s to O. B. Hardison, Jr.'s, study a hundred years later, there has been an effort to determine the potential for drama in the Mass and in the ceremonies surrounding the liturgical tropes.[2] The first Passion Play, as we shall see in a later chapter, differs significantly from its liturgical context; and one must look to other environments and other factors in order to understand the work. The immediate environment is the monastic culture of Montecassino in the twelfth century, and two factors seem to bear specifically on the composition of the Passion play. First, the choice of subject matter is decisive in a way not apparent in other medieval plays. The writer's decision to create a Passion drama obliges him to accommodate mimetic form to his topic, and the work must reflect the special features of the Passion itself. As G. J. Whitrow observes of Christianity, "Its central doctrine of the Crucifixion was regarded as a unique event in time not subject

---

2. Sepet's essays appeared in the *Bibliothèque de l'Ecole des Chartes* (1867–1878) and subsequently in *Les Prophètes du Christ: étude sur les origines du théâtre au Moyen âge* (Paris: Didier, 1878); O. B. Hardison, Jr., *Christian Rite and Christian Drama in the Middle Ages: Essays in the Origin and Early History of Modern Drama* (Baltimore: The Johns Hopkins Press, 1965). See E. Catherine Dunn, "Voice Structure in the Liturgical Drama: Sepet Reconsidered," in *Medieval English Drama*, pp. 44–63.

to repetition, and so implied that time must be linear and not cyclic."[3]

From the very outset, then, the dramatist faces a crucial limitation that involves the relation of aesthetics to doctrine. He cannot re-create the events of the Passion because his audience already perceives them as unable to be repeated. Instead, he has to devise a structure that allows a sense of recovery for the events that are now beyond repetition. This structure engages a particular act of imagination. It is unlike cultic imitation where the re-creating of Biblical events depends on the cyclicism and repetition of the liturgical forms. The audience postulated by Ethelwold's *Regularis Concordia*, for example, is able to repeat the emotions of the three Marys at the sepulchre; but the Cassinese audience remains at a distance from the action and so cannot imagine itself as duplicating the original emotions. The Passion dramatist attempts recovery under conditions of unity in which the unique and transcendent aspects of his topic take on a contemporary shape. In its full dimensions, the problem he faces is to define the nature of imitation in linear time.

The second important factor that bears on the play offers a practical solution to the problem of adapting dramatic form to the material. To establish a sense of recovery, the playwright relies on the drama's remarkable ability to transform space. His play changes the twelfth-century monastic setting to a concentrated image of the historical Jerusalem of the first century. Caiaphas' house, Gethsemane, the buildings of civil government, and Calvary replace the landmarks of the abbey and the *terra sancti Benedicti*. This ability to transform space distinguishes the drama from other genres that had taken up

3. G. J. Whitrow, *The Nature of Time* (New York: Holt, Rinehart, and Winston, 1972), p. 236.

the Passion theme. In the Middle Ages, narrative forms are equally capable of conveying the action of the Passion sequence. In both Latin and the vernacular languages, writers set down the events of suffering and Crucifixion. Works like the *Passion de Clermont-Ferrand*, the *Passion des jongleurs*, and the *Northern Passion* give the scenario a larger audience and an epic recounting. The events of the Passion can even be viewed synchronically through Gospel harmonies that correlate the narratives of the different Evangelists. In all these narratives, the action receives attention over the locales in which the Passion occurs.

In the lyric, Christian writers deal with other aspects of the Biblical material. The lyricists' stress is on an affective response to the Passion. The emotional interest of the poetry shifts from the action and its locales to concentrate on the speaker's own emotions. In a writer like Fortunatus, these emotions find their greatest expression. The opening stanzas of his "Vexilla regis" fuse images of the Passion and the speaker's emotions.

> The banners of the king advance,
> The cross with mystery doth flame,
> And from the tree the Flesh of flesh,
> Word Incarnate, hangs in shame.
>
> The lance's edge hath pierced his side,
> O look on Him that for our good
> Cleansed us of the stain of sin,
> Washed out with water and with blood.

Philip S. Allen points out that underneath the allegorical surface of these stanzas "Fortunatus' marching song of one Christian's faith is naive, instead of sentimental, appeals to

us as unpondered, immediate, real."[4] The Anglo-Saxon
Dream of the Rood similarly directs its tensions around images of the Crucifixion. By distancing the event through the
dreamer's memory and the Cross's own narration, the poem
draws attention to the human perspectives on the Crucifixion.[5]
The dramatist's inclusion of a *planctus* in the climactic scene
of the Passion play suggests his own recognition of these
qualities in the lyric.

The Montecassino playwright's emphasis on recovering a
particular, historical locale differs from the treatment of
space by the more familiar medieval dramatists of the vernacular tradition. The *Mystère de la Passion* played at Valen-
ciennes in 1547 attempts to reenact a larger story, and its
space consequently represents the known universe. The famous drawing preserved in the manuscript (Paris, Bibliothèque Nationale, MS. Français 12536, fols. 1^v–2–2bis) shows
settings not only for Jerusalem but also for the Church, Synagogue, Paradise, a room, Nazareth, the temple, the palace,
the bishops' house, the Golden Door, the ocean, Limbo, and
Hell. The English plays also adapt space to their specific
goals, although their scope is not as great as the vernacular
continental dramas and their techniques differ from those of
the Latin plays.[6] A primary difference between the twelfth-
century Passion dramatist and the fifteenth-century Wake-

4. Philip S. Allen, *The Romanesque Lyric: Studies in its Background and
Development from Petronius to the Cambridge Songs 50–1050* (1928; rpt.
New York: Barnes and Noble, 1969), p. 146; the translation is by Howard
Mumford Jones.
5. See Robert Edwards, "Narrative Technique and Distance in the *Dream
of the Rood*," *Papers on Language and Literature* 6 (1970), 291–301.
6. For recent discussions of staging in the English plays, see Stanley J.
Kahrl, *Traditions of Medieval English Drama* (London: Hutchinson Uni-
versity Library, 1974), pp. 27–52; Alan H. Nelson, *The Medieval English
Stage* (Chicago: The University of Chicago Press, 1974).

field Master is the latter's reliance on anachronism. By super-
imposing the Biblical landscape on the English countryside,
he stresses the ongoing importance of the Nativity. In the
Second Shepherds' Play, this confusion of past and present
allows the characters to reenact Christian mystery and to mix
the comic with the sublime.

The Montecassino dramatist's concern with history and
historical space connects his play to both the early traditions
of Christian writing and a contemporary interest in the Christian past at Montecassino. It is in these connections that one
can establish a useful context for composing the new work.
Erich Auerbach observes that one characteristic of Christian
writing is a concern with history. The details of everyday life,
the traits of ordinary individuals, and the features of common
places assume a prominence unimagined in classical writing.
Auerbach asserts that "from the outset Christianity was never
a mere doctrine or myth but was deeply involved in historical
existence. This is a significant, if not the most significant,
aspect of its specific character. On the one hand Christ became flesh in a definite historical situation, an earthly here and
now, in which he participated by his acts and his suffering—
while on the other hand, by thus atoning for Adam's guilt, he
restored man's share in the kingdom of God, which Adam
had lost."[7]

The joining of the historical to the transcendent requires
a particular orientation in Christian narrative. The New Testament writers are able to situate events naturalistically as a
way of underscoring the incarnational aspects of their dogma.

7. Erich Auerbach, *Literary Language and Its Public in Late Latin Antiquity and in the Middle Ages*, trans. Ralph Manheim, Bollingen Series, LXXIV
(New York: Pantheon Books, 1965), pp. 307–8.

In the writing of history itself, the nature of this orientation
becomes especially evident. For pagan historiography, Arnaldo Momigliano proposes that Thucydides may have been
the source for the idea that history "was a rhetorical work
with a maximum of invented speeches and a minimum of au-
thentic documents."[8] But in works like Eusebius' *Ecclesiastical History*, the rhetorical emphasis gives way to a stress on
documentation. The early Christian writers carry the insistence on historicity over to contemporary events. They attempt not only persuasion but also proof along the lines of
legal evidence. The documentation and proof in turn support
the larger plan of salvation. A Latin translation of the *Ecclesiastical History* by Rufinus made these practices and techniques available to writers in the West; in the eleventh century a transcription of Rufinus was made at Montecassino.[9]

In his own literary environment, the Passion dramatist
would have found a revived interest in historical writing.
Not only was Eusebius available, the *Annals* and *Histories*
of Tacitus had also come to Italy in the mid-eleventh century
with the German abbots of Montecassino.[10] The transcription
of other pagan writers like Apuleius, Terence, and Varro
during the eleventh and twelfth centuries parallels an interest
that centers on the Christian past. This second interest is apparent in the transcription of the *Peregrinatio Egeriae*, the
reconstruction of the basilica of St. Benedict under Desi-

8. Arnaldo Momigliano, "Pagan and Christian Historiography in the Fourth
Century A.D.," in *The Conflict between Paganism and Christianity in the
Fourth Century*, ed. Arnaldo Momigliano (Oxford: Clarendon Press, 1963),
p. 89.
9. *Codicum Casinensium Manuscriptorum Catalogus*, ed. Dom Mauro Inguanez (Montecassino: Badia, 1915), I, pt. 1, no. 95.
10. E. A. Lowe, *The Beneventan Script* (Oxford: Clarendon Press, 1914),
p. 11.

derius, and, in the age after Desiderius, in Peter the Deacon's *Liber de locis sanctis, Ortus et Vita Iustorum Cenobii Casinensis,* and his continuation of the *Chronicon* of Leo Marsicanus. The historical interest leads as well to the contemporary identification of the abbey as an allegorical Mount Sinai.

An anonymous eleventh-century poem in praise of Montecassino treats the connection between Sinai and the abbey as a matter of differing laws. Christian apologists had long seen the New Dispensation as a fulfillment of the Mosaic law, but the eleventh-century monastic writer goes even further to contrast the Ten Commandments and the Rule of St. Benedict.

Ritmus in Laudem Montis Casini

1. The law comes from Sinai and from Cassino; it is given to one and then the other by divine authority. The first is carved in a stone scroll; the other is painted in a vellum book.

2. The first law shows the hard hearts of the Jews; the one that succeeds it betokens the open character of the monks which, fed always on the law of the commandments, abounds with the fruits of good works.

3. Montecassino and Sinai are of equal value, each one answering to itself proportionally: thence the laws come forth, forbidding evil and giving different rewards for good works.

4. Sinai gives the Decalogue, Cassino the Rule. The mountain is not without grace; this wanderer lacks every care; the mountain is the valley of manna. Cassino is a mountain of glory and divine, too.

5. Sinai is in Arabia where Moses fasted and obtained the Decalogue; the true sun shone in his face and soon afterwards his likeness glowed like the sun.

6. The other Lawgiver, whom a reputation for abstinence made famous, lived in Cassino. His work never varied from his name; the native language gave him the name Benedict.

7. Then he was like Moses in splendor, seeing the King of all

kings in elegance. This labor finished and the toil, he gladly exchanged joys for hardship.

8. Montecassino rejoices in such a patron who deserved to sit in the twelfth seat and who shines in his crowned mitre. Lacking no good, he is its brightest jewel.

9. Sinai brought forth the law of the Israelites; the law of the cenacles came from Cassino. The first of them led to no one's perfection; the golden palace gives the second of them.[11]

The rhetorical strategy of the poem is nearly identical with its historical ideology. The major technique is opposition, and it pervades the ensemble of pastoral, legal, and apocalyptic motifs. The monks succeed the Israelites as the chosen people; they feed on the Commandments and surpass their prescriptions in good works. The fourth stanza is likely the most difficult passage, yet it reveals the peculiar force of historical analogy in the piece. The poet sets the Commandments against the Rule of St. Benedict and then turns to the imagery of Exodus. The wanderer mentioned is Moses, who is described as lacking every care (*caret omni carie*). The poet extends the similarities of *caret/carie* by using another sense of *caria*, 'bread,' in the phrase *carie mons Sinus*. He also plays on the resemblance between *Syna*, 'Sinai,' and *Sinus*, 'valley, gulf.' The reference here is to the manna that falls between Elim and Sinai (Exodus 16:4–35). The image of Moses as lawgiver dominates the rest of the poem. His transfiguration when he receives the Commandments becomes a prototype for Benedict's appearance in glory.

In the same century, Alphanus, the friend of Desiderius and later bishop of Salerno, returns to these motifs. His poem "De Casino monte" combines an evocation of the landscape

11. Text in *Miscellanea Cassinese*, no. 1 (1897), [p. 48].

with a description of the church. It also expands the possibility
of imaginative recovery by equating Montecassino with both
the Holy Land and heaven. At one point Alphanus says:

The palace of heaven lies open for virgins, widows, men, and spouses,
together with the holy orders. It used to be even more pious in works
and renowned in the monks. Behold, Cassino, the venerable mountain and palace of God, abounds in them. It is another Mount Sinai,
a guide for faith; this is the mountain where God bestowed the laws
to mankind, written with his own finger.[12]

The sort of antiquarianism that the playwright's contemporaries developed in writing about the Christian past differs
substantially from classical pagan antiquarianism. The ancient
writers derived names and social customs from the past and
often treated them as determinants of character. Varro derives the name Casinum from *cascum*, 'old,' and traces the
Samnites who inhabited the town back to the Sabines (*De
lingua latina*, VII, 29), but he is constrained to point out a
determinism in the fact that "even now we Romans call it the
Old Market." By contrast, the Christian writers see the past
as a model of what they want to return to. An idealization
of the locales and a nostalgia for earlier social forms run
through their writing. In these efforts at recovery, there is
also a sense of choice. No one is forced to dwell on the historical facets of the Holy Land or Montecassino; there is always
the alternative of concentrating on transcendent mysteries.
Hence one has to make a conscious decision to embrace the
reality of Christian antiquity. For the playwright, the general
willingness of his contemporaries to do so is a precondition
for a drama that would attempt to recover the historical
reality of the Passion.

12. Text in *Patrologia Latina*, ed. J.-P. Migne (Paris, 1879), CXLVII,
234–38.

The eleventh-century transcription of the *Peregrinatio Egeriae* preserves an early example of Christian antiquarianism and could have provided Cassinesi writers a model for such works. This fourth-century report of a Spanish nun's pilgrimage to the holy places records some of the earliest information about liturgical practices in the Eastern church and in the Jerusalem rite. It seeks as well to describe the monuments of the Christian past and to convey their reality to a monastic audience as removed in space from the major shrines as the dramatist's audience is removed in time from the events of the Passion. Egeria's preoccupation is solely with the evidence of Biblical history. Harry J. Leon notes, "She has no interest whatever in the imposing pagan monuments, which she must have seen. She does not refer to the customs and activities of the people in the cities and villages through which she passed. Only occasionally does she allude to natural scenery, and then in the briefest terms. Her concern is only with biblical associations and with religious practices. Although she quotes frequently from the Bible, there is never a reference to a pagan author."[13] Throughout her report, Egeria maintains a dual focus. She is conscious of both the "dominae sorores" to whom she speaks directly and the intersection of her experience with the scenes of Christian history.

The commemorations Egeria observes at the shrines repeatedly merge the present with the recovered past. For instance, after climbing Mount Sinai, which the Cassinesi would identify with their own monastery, she reports, "there is nothing there except a single church and the cave where the holy Moses was. Having read through the Book of Moses

13. Harry J. Leon, "A Medieval Nun's Diary," *Classical Journal* 59 (1963), 123.

in this place and made the offerings to us as communicants according to their custom, the priests gave us gifts, that is, some fruit that grows on the mountain itself, as we were leaving the church."[14] The readings and communion do not abolish Egeria's experience as a pilgrim so much as frame it in a larger context. The social acts of welcome and exchange exist alongside the commemoration. Her description expresses this coexistence to an audience that remains distant from the locales. For the audience, the writing permits an imaginative approach to the scenes.

In her descriptions, Egeria develops rhetorical techniques especially suited to conveying her impressions of the Biblical locales. Like the dramatist, she must treat this space in a compelling and persuasive way. Leo Spitzer maintains that the forms she uses anticipate the stylistic features of medieval Romance poetry. Her repetitions are devices for prolonging scenes and giving them an emotional emphasis. The repetitions also have a function in testimony, and Spitzer believes that "she is surely 'legalistic' in the precision with which she attempts to identify relics and places." To the extent that repetition retards the development of narrative, "this literary technique reflects the new Christian technique of life, which enjoins the believer to keep before his eyes, at any moment and in any situation, the significance of life under the New Dispensation."[15] The rhetorical monotony of her style thus halts the linear flow of time. The stylistic and structural repetitions

14. *Peregrinatio Sylviae*, in *Itinera Hierosolymitana, Saeculi IIII–VIII*, ed. Paul Geyer, Corpus Scriptorum Ecclesiasticorum Latinorum, XXXIX (1898; rpt. New York: Johnson Reprint Corp., 1964), p. 40. I have followed recent scholarship in preferring the name Egeria to Sylvia or Etheria.

15. Leo Spitzer, "The Epic Style of the Pilgrim Aetheria," *Comparative Literature* 1 (1949), 231, 234.

allow her readers the sense of recovery that she feels on her own journey.

To the dramatist attempting to devise his own conventions for representing Christian history, Egeria's narrative would be instructive in several respects. First, it would teach him the purpose of depicting the areas where his action is to occur. His aim in re-creating an historical space is not to reproduce the scenes in complete detail. Rather, he would want to create an atmosphere of authenticity to complement his documentary style of exposition. Second, Egeria's account would demonstrate the special features of writing for a monastic audience. The author can assume a greater uniformity than in other audiences, and he can rely on a common range of reference. Third, Egeria could show the dramatist how to structure the re-creation of different locales around an action. The action of her pilgrimage connects the various sites she describes. In the drama, a movement through various acting areas would adopt a similar pattern.

In the century following the transcription of the *Peregrinatio*, Peter the Deacon's *Liber de locis sanctis* (c. 1137) deals with the recovery of space under conditions somewhat closer to those faced by the dramatist. Peter's book is a compilation based on Egeria and on the Venerable Bede's own *Liber de locis sanctis*, whose transcription Desiderius had ordered.[16] The absence of firsthand reporting distinguishes Peter's work from Egeria's record. Her presence at the shrines permits the nun to argue from experience, and cen-

---

16. Dom Mauro Inguanez, "Il Venerabile Beda nei codici e negli scrittori cassinesi medievali," *Studia Anselmiana* 6 (1936), 44; Leo Marsicanus, *Chronicon Casinense*, III. 63.

turies of tradition lend credibility to her narrative. Peter relies
partly on such tradition in characterizing his work as a collection of existing documents and hence as a work based on
authority. Yet the burden of persuasion in the book rests prin-
cipally on techniques of description. His major device for
persuasion is measurement, the translation of space into
known and objective mathematical units. Egeria and Bede
occasionally use the device for their documents of the holy
places, but in Peter's book the concept of measurement takes
on different features from the earlier records.

Bede, who depends on a similar work written by the Irish
priest Adamnanus in the seventh century, sets down two
varieties of measurement. He measures discrete objects in
space and the distance between the objects. By linking the
size of the monuments to their positioning, he attempts to
synthesize the two kinds of measurement. In this effort, he
introduces a tendency toward compression into the narrative;
the descriptions seem to concentrate the areas of geographical
space. Peter's book gives less attention to measuring geo-
metrical forms. Instead, it focuses on the second variety of
measurement—the relative positions of the places. The references to Sichem in Bede and Peter illustrate their different
narrative procedures. Bede writes, "Near the city of Sichem,
which is now called Neopolis, there is a four-sided church
made in the shape of a cross; in its middle is the fountain of
Jacob, forty cubits high measured from one's side to the far-
thest extended finger, from which the Lord deigned to ask
water from the Samaritan woman."[17] Peter's interest is in
portraying a landscape rather than describing objects. Peter
locates the forms in such a way that the dimensions of space
become the dominant feature of the narrative. He says, "This

17. Bede, *Liber de locis sanctis*, in *Itinera Hierosolymitana*, p. 319.

Aesthetics of Recovery

church is two miles distant from that place which was once called Sichem. Fifty feet from this church is another in which the blessed Joseph rests."[18]

The measurements of Peter's *Liber de locis sanctis* are part of a rhetorical strategy. The mathematics asserts the credibility of his descriptions and links them to the antiquarian descriptions of Christian writers and even the Old Testament. The internal system of spatial relationships is fundamental to his descriptions. By tradition, Jerusalem and the outlying places are sacred space and constitute the *axis mundi*. They cannot be defined from external points of reference; and when the playwright comes to re-create this space, he will maintain its hermetic quality, even to the point of staging Judas' suicide outside the acting area. Bede seems to recognize the inadequacy of external measurement and attempts to overcome the tendency toward compressing the area by defining a cubit as the distance between one's side and the finger of an outstretched arm. Yet even that definition can only be approximate since the distance will vary among individuals. Peter seems more willing to accept the tendency toward a compressed description. By stressing the positioning of objects rather than their surface dimensions, he makes the descriptions nearly iconographical. In iconography the representation necessarily deals with the relative placement of objects in a scene. As the media vary between miniatures, textiles, or monuments, the placement of different objects remains generally constant.

The concentration of space in Peter's descriptions implies a further imaginative treatment of the shrines and holy places. The writing employs a system of internal relationships like

18. Peter the Deacon, *Liber de locis sanctis*, in *Itinera Hierosolymitana*, p. 112.

that developed in Antiquity by the art of memory and transmitted to the Middle Ages as part of rhetorical training. In mnemonics, a series of objects is committed to memory by imagining a superimposed grid or Memory House whose individual sections (*stanze*) would contain an object (*topos*). Numbered sequentially, each section would call up the one adjoining it, and by such a progression the objects in them could be recalled. Like Peter's descriptions, this system takes no account of the surface dimensions of the objects. Any object may be fitted imaginatively in a section, and the division into sections is wholly artificial.[19] For the antiquarian writer, these techniques would let him connect the distinctive features of the landscape without regard for scale or dimension. The shrines thus appear contiguous, and the gaps that intervene between them do nothing to offset the intensity of imagining the scenes. For the dramatist, movement between the different locales might suggest the arrangement of multiple mansion staging in which various acting areas lie next to each other and the actors shift from one scene to another. Onstage as in the narrative descriptions, one experiences the monuments and historical sites in a continual progression.

The effects of miniature and mnemonics redirect the historical emphases of antiquarian writing and the drama by establishing an affective basis for them. Modern theorists point out that the connections between historical scenes and miniatures involve more than a simple correspondence. Gaston Bachelard cautions one away from "Platonic dialectics of large and small," claiming that they "do not suffice for us to become cognizant of the dynamic virtue of miniature

19. For a detailed discussion of mnemonics, see Frances Yates, *The Art of Memory* (Chicago: The University of Chicago Press, 1966).

thinking."[20] Claude Lévi-Strauss argues that the dynamics of miniature involve special features. Miniatures are manmade; they represent genuine confrontations with objects in nature and "they are therefore not just projections or passive homologues of the object; they constitute a real experiment with it."[21] The nature of this experiment is toward the intelligible. As T. S. Eliot might say, miniatures "objectify" experience by translating it to another form. They isolate items from the ongoing flow of life so that the items appear holistic, fixed, and permanent. Miniature thus allows an approach to the past through a kind of mental traveling.

The description of space in Peter's *Liber de locis sanctis* assures the further possibility of recovering it in time. One aligns the space of Christian antiquity with the inner space of belief. Among modern thinkers, Bachelard points out a similar treatment of space. He observes, "Space that has been seized upon by the imagination cannot remain indifferent space subject to the measures and estimates of the surveyor. It has been lived in, not in its positivity, but with all the partiality of the imagination. Particularly, it nearly always exercises an attraction. For it concentrates being within limits that protect. In the realm of images, the play between the exterior and intimacy is not a balanced one."[22] In the following chapter, we shall examine the playwright's reliance on miniatures as a way of portraying his transcendent subject and composing specific scenes in the work. Here it is enough to recognize that a work like Peter's book signals a general concern

20. Gaston Bachelard, *The Poetics of Space*, trans. Maria Jolas (New York: Orion Press, 1964), p. 150.
21. Claude Lévi-Strauss, *The Savage Mind* (Chicago: The University of Chicago Press, 1966), p. 24.
22. Bachelard, *The Poetics of Space*, p. xxxii.

at Montecassino in the twelfth century with treating the locales of Christian history imaginatively. For his own aesthetic
aims, the Passion dramatist will re-create some of these same
locales. Just as Peter's book links the reader to the holy places,
the Passion drama will connect its audience to the Biblical
events.

These innovations in descriptive practices and the special
concern with recovery appear against a larger backdrop. The
emphasis on recovery shows itself in various forms of the cultural life of Montecassino. The reconstruction of the basilica,
the arrival of relics, and the ceremonies of communal life are
related to the literary developments. The intentions behind
these various facets, it should be noted, are not simply devotional. The nature of devotion is to separate the emotional
and spiritual from everyday life and collective experience.
Neither are the intentions predominantly moral, as in the
civic entertainments that use drama in the later Middle Ages
to address the individual sinner and urge his reform. The
intentions, rather, are social. The efforts at recovery aim to
recast everyday life in the models of earlier, historical experience. Such ambitions may have been possible only in a
monastic community like Montecassino which enjoyed both
a spiritual unity and an extraordinary awareness of its past.
Seen in these contexts, the first Passion play loses its anoma-
lous character as an isolated text. One can view it instead as
part of a conscious social movement.

The reconstruction of the basilica under Desiderius provides its own evidence of a conscious effort to recover the
monuments of Christian antiquity. The church is a synthesis
of two distinct styles and ecclesiastical traditions. Herbert
Bloch observes that "while the architecture of the church is

Aesthetics of Recovery

western in origin and character, its decoration was done under the direction of Byzantine artists." When Desiderius began the reconstruction, "he not only ordered works of art in Constantinople, but he also summoned thence a great number of artists, both to execute works themselves and to teach the monks the arts in which the Byzantines were supposed to be the greatest masters of their time." These artists were involved in restoring traditional forms of expression, thereby enabling the monks to regain lost skills in fashioning images from mosaics, marble, gold, silver, bronze, iron, glass, ivory, wood, alabaster, and stone. In the *Chronicon* (III. 27) Leo Marsicanus uses the verb *recuperare*, 'to recover, to gain back,' to characterize Desiderius' motive in directing a number of the younger monks to seek instruction from the Byzantines. "And since *magistra Latinitas* had left uncultivated the practice of these arts for more than five hundred years, and through the efforts of this man, with the inspiration and help of God, promised to regain it in our time, the abbot in his wisdom decided that a great number of young monks in the monastery should be thoroughly initiated in these arts in order that their knowledge might not again be lost in Italy."[23]

The finished basilica was one of the marvels of the High Middle Ages, but it represents more than an archeological achievement. The achievement has its social result as well, for the combination of Eastern and Western elements suggests a movement past the contemporary division in the church to a united Christian community. That a church should furnish the image for this recovery is consistent with a common attitude in ecclesiastical thinking. George Every says,

23. Herbert Bloch, "Monte Cassino, Byzantium, and the West in the Earlier Middle Ages," in *Dumbarton Oaks Papers*, no. 3 (1946), pp. 196, 194; the translation is by Bloch.

"In the Byzantine view the church itself was a symbol, like the Tabernacle and the Temple as they are described in *Exodus* and the *Second Book of Chronicles*, for the Byzantines inherited from the early church an idea of art that is unhellenic. Their pagan borrowings were in the details; the frame was Biblical, a representation in earthly, visible materials of an invisible, heavenly pattern, revealed to the eye of faith upon the mount of God. In some Rabbinical interpretations, followed by the author of the *Epistle to the Hebrews*, the pattern is the plan of the heavenly temple."[24] Rabanus Maurus, whose *De universo* was transcribed at Montecassino in about 1023, cites *Exodus* to the same effect, saying that the temple, a figure of the Church, "as soon as it was set down in its homeland and built in the royal city on sacred ground, fulfilled the function of arraying itself as a figure of the heavens; in it, the labor and exile of the present Church, the future repose and blessedness can be prefigured."[25]

As a transcendent image of the heavens, the reconstructed basilica loses none of its historical associations. The structure returns the community to the origins of Western monasticism in the era of St. Benedict and so remedies the disruptions occasioned by the Lombard invasion of 581 and the Saracen attack of 883, which devastated the abbey. Peter the Deacon's *Ortus et vita* (LVIII) ascribes the recovery to a vision Desiderius had sometime after entering the monastery. He reports that "there appeared to him a vision that is not to be valued lightly. He saw himself in the tower that used to stand next to the chapter house, and in which father Benedict was clearly

24. George Every, *The Byzantine Patriarchate 451–1204*, 2nd ed. (London: SPCK, 1962), p. 80.

25. Rabanus Maurus, *De universo*, xxii. 21, in *Patrologia Latina*, CXI, 393.

seen sitting in a most fitting chair. And since he was terrified by this vision and dumbfounded, and in no way could take a step to come closer, the blessed father Benedict cheerfully nodded to him and with an extended hand bade him sit next to him. The outcome of things proved the vision. Made abbot soon afterward, he renovated the monastery just as it is seen now.''[26]

The renovated basilica marks an even further approach to recovery by evoking the sense of a unified church supported by a Roman Christian Emperor. Constantine had inscribed the major arch of the Lateran basilica, *Quod duce te mundus surrexit in astra triumphans / Hanc Constantinus victor tibi condidit aulam* ('Because while you are lord the world rose triumphing into the heavens, Constantine the victor built this palace for you.') For the basilica of St. Benedict, Desiderius ordered a similar inscription in gold letters: *Ut duce te patria justis potiatur adepta, / Hanc Desiderius pater hanc tibi condidit aulam* ('So that, while you are lord, the fatherland might have the proper observances, the father Desiderius built this palace for you.')[27] Desiderius' inscription images the historical space of the abbey in an era when the church first aligns itself with imperial power and secular institutions. It thus makes possible an imaginative act in which the present community can see itself in the models of earlier Christians.

The social movement toward recovery would find additional support in yet another facet of the contemporary interest

---

26. *Petri Diaconi: Ortus et Vita Iustorum Cenobii Casinensis*, ed. R. H. Rodgers, University of California Publications: Classical Studies, X (Berkeley: University of California Press, 1972), p. 78.

27. Leo Marsicanus, *Chronicon*, III. 28. The similarities are pointed out by Ambrogio Amelli, "La Basilica di Montecassino e la Lateranese nel secolo XI," in *Miscellanea Cassinese*, no. 1 (1897), pp. 16–20.

in Christian antiquities. The relics of the Biblical past strength-
en the part of recovered time. They are not symbolic in the
sense that, like Desiderius' inscription, they represent something else. The relics are themselves portions of Christian history; they are direct evidence for the events recounted in the
gospels and commemorated in liturgy. Montecassino was particularly fortunate in the matter of relics. The Norman Robert
Guiscard donated the arm of St. Matthew. The monk Leon,
returning from Jerusalem in the late tenth century, brought
a substantial piece of the cross with him. In 1023, Pope Benedict VIII donated another piece of the cross. In Desiderius'
abbacy, a noble returning from Constantinople offered a piece
of the cross stolen from the imperial palace. Later inventories
mention the abbey's having a piece of the column where Christ
was bound, a piece of his robe, and some of the thorns. The
monastery also owned a piece of the cloth used for washing
the apostles' feet at the Last Supper.[28] Thus by the twelfth
century, the abbey possessed relics for the major events of
the Passion. In the observances for Holy Week, these relics
would assume a special prominence as objects of commemoration and worship. They would offer an historical basis for
rituals that had grown up later to celebrate the Passion and
Resurrection.

The ceremonies of monastic life provide an additional link
with the historical models of early Christianity. Whereas the
imaginative treatment of space and the possession of relics allow projections back in time, the ceremonies give an exterior
and tangible form to the images of the past. They also add a
mimetic element to the recovery of Christian history. One

28. Dom Mauro Inguanez, "Reliquie della Passione a Montecassino," *Illu-
strazione Vaticana* 5 (1934), 315–16.

not only visualizes the space of the Holy Land, as in Peter's *Liber de locis sanctis*, but also reenacts the events that occurred there. In this respect the ceremonies may approach the cultic imitation of the early liturgical drama. However, the documentary emphasis of the period makes impossible the ready identification of the community with Biblical characters. In the fourth chapter, we shall examine the connections between liturgical forms and the drama. For the moment, it is important to realize that the ceremonies share with the other facets of recovery an awareness of their own historical basis.

For twelfth-century Montecassino, the immediate sources for the ceremonies reach back to rites in the Roman and Jerusalem churches. The introduction of these sources changes and amplifies the observances laid down originally by St. Benedict during the first half of the sixth century in his *Regula Monachorum*. A ceremony like the washing of the feet, outlined in chapters 35 and 53 of the *Regula* for the community and visitors respectively, endures in twelfth-century Holy Week ritual as the Mandatum. Nonetheless, the observances increasingly derive from the practices of the early Jerusalem church and appear in Roman rite generally after the tenth century. The sources of the ceremonies again point up the historical process. The ritual observances are supported by the weight of authority and tradition, but they remain as evidence of Christian antiquity.

The incorporation of the Jerusalem ceremonies into medieval structures pushes backward in time Erwin Panofsky's view that "no medieval man could see the civilization of antiquity as a phenomenon complete in itself, yet belonging to the past and historically detached from the contemporary world,—as a cultural cosmos to be investigated and, if possible to be reintegrated, instead of being a world of living wonders or a mine of information."[29] The civilization Montecassino looked to was Christian, not pagan; and the incorporation of it could be possible only under the conditions that Panofsky describes as "renaissance." E. I. Watkin has already argued an earlier date for this perspectival view of history. He suggests that in order to conquer the world, the church had to stoop to the world and that "she has never ceased to look back wistfully to the days when, as a persecuted minority, she could stand erect with head unbowed."[30] Watkin sees the move toward monastic life in the Middle Ages as a return to the conclaves of early Christian worship.

In a ceremony like the procession for Palm Sunday, the attempts at recovery encompass both sacred and ecclesiastical history. At Montecassino after Terce the priests, deacons, and subdeacons vest themselves in stoles and maniples. Following the cross, they proceed two by two out of St. Benedict, the principal church, to the church of St. Stephen or St. Martin, singing the antiphon "Cum audisset populus." Behind them in the procession are two acolytes with candelabra and two with thuribles, two deacons, two subdeacons and finally the abbot wearing a chasuble. Arriving at the church, the chorus begins to sing the antiphon "Hosanna filio David" as the ministers approach the altar to recite prayers and read Matthew's account of the entry into Jerusalem (Matthew 21: 1–11). Immediately after this reading, the palms and olive branches are blessed and distributed; the community then re-

29. Erwin Panofsky, *Studies in Iconology* (New York: Harper Torchbooks, 1962), p. 27.

30. E. I. Watkin, *Catholic Art and Culture* (New York: Sheed and Ward, 1944), p. 13. See also Walter Ullmann, *The Individual and Society in the Middle Ages* (Baltimore: The Johns Hopkins Press, 1966), pp. 101–51.

turns to the church of St. Benedict, singing antiphons that recall the New Testament account. At the door of the church three clerics exchange verses with the procession. The clerics end the exchange by singing, "As the Lord was entering the Holy City, the Hebrew children with palm branches, announcing the resurrection of the life, cried, 'Hosanna in the highest.'" Afterward the procession begins to enter the church, repeating the clerics' verses.[31]

The structure, hymnody, and action of these ceremonies dramatize the events that precede the Passion. The procession to the minor church recalls Christ's journey to Mt. Olivet with the disciples, and the return to St. Benedict symbolizes the entry into Jerusalem. At the same time, the recovery of sacred time and space involves an awareness of the ceremonies in church history. Egeria reports that the people of Jerusalem journey to Mt. Olivet singing hymns. With the arrival of the bishop, hymns, antiphons, lessons, and prayers are read there. After the reading of Matthew's gospel, the people reply with antiphons and then, holding palms and olive branches, they lead the bishop through the city.[32] Egeria does not record the blessing of the palms and olive branches, which seems to be a monastic development and first appears in the seventh-century Bobbio Missal. Yet even with this later innovation, the process of recovery implies a synthesis of Scripture and Christian antiquarianism. As an early community of believers, the people of Jerusalem provide an additional model of devotion to which the twelfth-century Cassinesi return by imitation. The procession to the minor church and the subsequent

31. *Ordo Casinensis Hebdomadae Maioris (saec. xii)*, ed. Teodoro Leuterman, in *Miscellanea Cassinese*, no. 20 (1941), pp. 19, 96–97. Hereafter cited as *Ordo*.

32. *Peregrinatio Sylviae*, in *Itinera Hierosolymitana*, pp. 83–84.

return to St. Benedict occupy sacred space in the same manner as Egeria's ascent of Mt. Olivet and her later entry into the Holy City with the procession.

In the case of the Holy Thursday ceremonies, the concern with the Christian past refers the community back to its own early practices. The Mandatum takes place at Terce after the celebration of the Missa pauperibus, and the abbot joins the community in washing the feet of poor people brought into the church. After Vespers another version of the Mandatum, under the title Sermo Dominicus, is carried out for the community. The twelfth-century Ordo states the connection between the Biblical incident and the ceremony. "Then, after the brothers have eaten what was set before them but not quite consuming an entire meal, let them in imitation of the Savior all rise at a silent signal from the prior. Going into the chapter house, let everyone—the abbot and the various brothers—wash in turn each other's feet."[33] In Benedict's *Regula*, the community would find further parallels for the ceremonies. The Holy Thursday Mandatum is a stylized version of the observance for guests set down in chapter 53 of the *Regula*: "Let the abbot give the guests water for their hands; and let both abbot and community wash the feet of all guests. When they have washed them, let them say this verse: *Suscepimus, Deus, misericordiam tuam in medio templi tui*. In the reception of poor men and pilgrims special attention should be shown, because in them is Christ more truly welcomed; for the fear which the rich inspire is enough of itself to secure them honour." The Sermo Dominicus enacts in Passiontide the kind of ceremony held when members of the community begin and end weekly service in the kitchen. The *Regula* prescribes, "both the servers, that is, the server

33. *Ordo*, pp. 103–4.

who is ending his week and he who is about to begin, shall wash the feet of the whole community."[34]

The social nature of the drama seems to connect innovations in form to particular cultural contexts. For early Greek tragedy, Gerald Else stresses the impact of social conditions that made Athens the guardian of a cultural heritage after the Persian War. He sees the classical drama's preoccupation with heroic myths as an attempt to regain the values of the Homeric age. As a result, the form of classical drama revolves around "the hero's view of himself and the chorus' view of him." Else says, "The hero is the fulcrum of the whole. Without him there would be no tragedy, or none worth having. But without the chorus there would not be any tragedy either; the hero would be suspended in a vacuum with no sounding board to respond to his passion and no separate standard by which to measure him. Thus the original form of tragedy—single actor and chorus—established a tension which is of its essence."[35] The drama of the later Middle Ages reflects another sort of connection between drama and its social context. F. M. Salter traces the earliest English mystery cycles to the economic and social life at Chester in the last quarter of the fourteenth century. The division of the Biblical material into separate plays accords with the growing prestige of trade and religious guilds, and the visual opulence of the plays requires their financial support.[36] As Glynne Wickham observes, "From the outset the drama associated

---

34. *The Rule of St. Benedict*, ed. and trans. Justin McCann (Westminster, Maryland: The Newman Press, 1952), pp. 120, 89.

35. Gerald Else, *The Origin and Early Form of Greek Tragedy*, Martin Classical Lectures, XX (Cambridge, Mass.: Harvard University Press, 1967), p. 44.

36. F. M. Salter, *Mediaeval Drama in Chester* (Toronto: University of Toronto Press, 1955).

with Corpus Christi was directed towards the frivolous rich and the covetous tradesmen in an effort to rededicate society to Christ and Christ's service in the remembrance that Christ had died to save mankind."[37]

In its structure of values, twelfth-century Montecassino is as different from medieval Chester as it is from classical Athens. Its society is closed and fixed by the models laid down by St. Benedict in his Rule. Its economies follow the pattern of Roman landholdings and feudal privilege, and there is no class of men emerging as new claimants to power. The social institutions of monasticism lend a stability that endures through various reforms from the sixth century to Francis of Assisi's attempts to redefine the character of monastic life in the thirteenth century. More than anything else, Montecassino's own sense of place shapes its distinctive values. Although Athens stands over a Greek cultural heritage, that heritage is not specifically Athenian. Chester may present an extraordinary case of civic unity and development, but it has no particular historical continuity to look back on.

By contrast, Montecassino's history encompasses both the general history of mankind and the individual history of one place. Christian antiquarianism deals with the evidence of this general history in terms accessible to everyone. It recreates the original site of Biblical events and asserts a transcendent value. In this way, the abbey like any other religious community can see itself as an allegorical Mount Sinai. Yet from the time of Gregory the Great's *Dialogues*, Montecassino receives special attention as the origin of Western monasticism. A dominant theme of Cassinese social life in the eleventh and twelfth centuries is to return to these images of the Biblical

37. Glynne Wickham, *The Medieval Theatre* (New York: St. Martin's Press, 1974), p. 65.

and ecclesiastical past as means of recovering history from time. The transcription and composition of works on the Holy Land, the acquisition of relics, and the innovations in liturgy point up the attempt to regain the Biblical past. At the same time, the abbey remains conscious of its own past. In contemporary writing and art, Desiderius appears as a second Benedict. His reconstruction of the basilica accordingly marks a return to the abbey's founding. This interest continues beyond Desiderius' own age and into the twelfth century when figures like Peter the Deacon attempt to recapture the monastery's sense of its eminence.

These social values provide a wider context for understanding the Passion play and its aesthetics. The drama's focus on transcendence and history owes to doctrinal views of the Passion. But the playwright's contemporaries would have recognized a similar dualism in their own preoccupations with allegory and historical analogy. In this respect, the abbey's larger concerns complement the theoretical aspects of a Passion drama. The writing of his contemporaries might also influence the dramatist in some of his techniques. Antiquarian literature would teach him the importance of space in an imaginative treatment of the past. Moreover, it would demonstrate the value of combining Biblical and apocryphal material to create persuasive evidence. In all these connections, the play affirms the ties to its age.

3. The Passion Play and the Visual Arts

ART HISTORIANS in this century have recognized an important connection between the early medieval drama and the visual arts. In particular they stress the impact of the liturgical drama on the iconographical programs of Romanesque and Gothic art. Emile Mâle finds evidence of a connection in the twelfth century when the *Visitatio Sepulchri* provides new motifs for artists depicting the Resurrection and the Christmas drama inspires representations of the Magi. Other works like the Anglo-Norman *Jeu d'Adam* and a similar play from Rouen influence the portrayal of the prophets, a favorite topic in Italian ecclesiastical art. In southern France, the *Sponsus* from Limoges influences pictorial renderings of the parable of the Wise and Foolish Virgins (Matthew 25:1–13).[1] Otto Pächt finds the impact of the drama on art in such developments as the representation of a liturgical *sepulchrum* for the tomb mentioned in scriptural sources, the expansion of figures at the Nativity to include the midwives, and even the "style of narrative" in the Emmaus miniatures of the St. Albans Psalter.[2]

An emergent dramatic form, however, requires an almost

1. Emile Mâle, *L'art religieux du XIIe Siècle en France*, 3rd ed. (Paris: Librairie Armand Colin, 1928), pp. 121–50.
2. Otto Pächt, *The Rise of Pictorial Narrative in Twelfth-Century England* (Oxford: Clarendon Press, 1962), pp. 28–41.

opposite recurrence to already established genres. The language and rubrics of the Montecassino Passion play suggest this direction by attempting to convey the action of the Passion as a series of visual images. In addition, the speeches and choral addresses of the play frequently serve as glosses on dramatic action. A close reading of the text thus indicates an important link between the composition of the play and the visual arts. In its major aspects, this connection involves two distinct areas of influence. First, the playwright would rely on traditional attitudes toward the visual arts as a way of representing his transcendent subject matter. The play becomes a counterpart to the miniature cycle, and it follows the same ideological lines that had earlier been laid down for images. Second, the play relies on iconographical sources for composing specific scenes of the drama. These sources do not reflect only the general pictorial conventions of Christian art; they also reflect the specific cultural interchange between East and West that brought Byzantine models of depiction to Western art.

The drama's use of the visual arts draws by analogy on the general defense of images by the Eastern Church Fathers. As Ernst Kitzinger points out, before the second half of the fourth century Christian art had been a natural, unquestioned extension of pagan and Jewish art. In that century, Gregory of Nyssa responded to Julian the Apostate's attack on Christian liturgical art with the argument that Christians were no more than paying "the customary honors of the sovereign" in honoring the saints. Their adoration "received in their statues and pictures" might enlist a veneration "more insatiable and more complete" than they would otherwise gain. At Constantinople in 692, the Quinisext Council passed judgment in its 82nd Canon on the matter of representation, particularly as it applied to Christ depicted as a lamb. The Council held that the symbolism should be replaced by representations of Christ in human form "so that we may perceive through it the depth of the humiliation of God the Word and be led to the remembrance of His life in the flesh, His Passion and His death, and of the redemption which it brought into the world."[3] In 767 the Second Council of Nicaea reaffirmed the sanction of anthropomorphic images. Common in these sanctions is reference to Genesis 1:27 where man is said to be created in God's image. From this scriptural basis, the apologists establish an image-prototype relationship between God, men, and visual images.

In the West, the most influential defense of images appears in Gregory the Great's two letters to Serenus, the bishop of Marseilles. Gregory admonishes Serenus not to destroy images within the churches, and in both letters he distinguishes adoration of the images from instruction. In the second letter he says, "for it is one thing to adore a picture and quite another to learn from narrative paintings what should be adored. For what a book is to those who can read, a picture provides to even the unlearned who look at it carefully, for in it the unlearned see what they should follow, and those who cannot read books read it. Hence a picture especially serves as a book to the common people." Gregory's idea that the images were a book for the common people informs most subsequent thinking on the matter. Rosemary Woolf observes, "From the early twelfth century onwards the view that images served as *libri laicorum* became so widespread that it would be impossible to enumerate all those who expounded it."[4]

3. Ernst Kitzinger, "The Cult of Images in the Age before Iconoclasm," in *Dumbarton Oaks Papers*, no. 8 (1954), pp. 91, 121.

4. Rosemary Woolf, *The English Mystery Plays* (Berkeley: University of California Press, 1972), pp. 87–88; the translation is by Woolf (p. 365n).

The defense of images in late Antiquity extends not only to church decoration but also to relics and icons. The unique image-prototype relation that relics assumed has much to do with the miraculous and magical powers they acquired first as the actual remains of saints and then later as depictions of them. Both kinds of relics are, in Kitzinger's phrase, "material props" which anticipate the influences later ascribed to other visual images. The relics find their religious impetus not in any special sanctions by the church but in the miracles performed in their name or in their presence. The secular impetus for relics comes "through the symbolic identification of the instrument of Christ's passion with the victorious standard of the army of Constantine the Great, an identification graphically expressed in the sign of the labarum, which appears on coins in the third decade of the fourth century."[5] The typology of Christ as Emperor further indicates a recovery of time. The labarum recalls the transcendent action of redemption through suffering, while it associates the divine and secular rulers. Thus the image tends to confuse the divine realm and the worldly state. So long as the relic is only a reminder of divine power, this confusion raises no theological issues. But when, as in the case of miracle stories, the image in fact controls the action or acts as the figure it depicts might have acted, then questions of idolatry begin to appear.

The justifications of icons follow similar lines to the defense of relics, but a difference begins to emerge between the two. Kitzinger maintains that "the pictorial rendering of the living form was able to inherit the virtues of the relic and to gain an equal, and eventually more than equal, importance." Commenting on Gregory of Nyssa's defense of the relics in

5. Kitzinger, "The Cult of Images in the Age before Iconoclasm," pp. 89–90.

the Encomium of St. Theodore, he suggests, "In this ecstatic passage, in which the shapeless relic is merely a tool for conjuring up the physical presence of a saint, one can discern something of the roots of future image worship. For if a sensual perception of the living form is the devout's primary need, it is obvious that the work of the painter and sculptor can be of greater assistance to him than a handful of dust and bones." The justifications for icons in churches and homes eventually came to be fourfold. The earliest use of them is didactic. As Gregory the Great shows in his letters to Serenus, the icons were a way of teaching those who could not read. They could also be used to "challenge those whose christological views were not in agreement with orthodox dogma." With Gregory of Nyssa, emotion becomes a factor. As the images begin to appear in marketplaces and private dwellings in addition to churches, magic becomes their prevalent justification. Miracle stories and popular devotion assert the thaumaturgic power of the icons. Finally, with the Pseudo-Dionysus, a Neoplatonic rationale evolves. Pseudo-Dionysus saw the spiritual and material realms as superimposed images of one another; "the entire world of the senses in all its variety reflects the world of the spirit. Contemplation of the former serves as a means to elevate ourselves toward the latter."[6] With this last justification, a transcendent element could be superimposed onto the historical element.

The practice of book illustration carries these ideas about visual images even closer to the drama since, as we shall see, the Passion drama shows a correlation with the iconography of miniature cycles. Classical writers mention that portraits of authors are included on the frontispieces of their works. Illus-

6. Ibid., pp. 116, 121, 138.

trations also survive from late Antiquity for portions of the *Iliad* and *Aeneid*.[7] Still, the classical period generally considered the book as a vehicle for conveying thought. The system of enlarged titles and initials developed by Greek and Roman scribes existed as a practical aid to readers, to help them find information. The size of the script increased, though the letters retained their normal shapes. Only when the book began to lose its function as a message-bearer and gain in value as an object of ornamentation or cult was greater care taken in its copying, decoration, and binding. The texts were then given special attention; and the binding boards, too, were enriched. In these instances, the decoration had no other aim than embellishment. The attempt was to make the works more valuable and, in the case of holy books, to render them more worthy of veneration. In Italy, in the fourth century, initials first began to receive decoration and color. Within a century the modestly ornamental book of Antiquity had become the wonderfully ornate medieval book.

As in the carry-over of images from pre-Christian into Christian culture, there seems to have been no need by scribes to formulate an explicitly Christian apology for illustration except as an adjunct to the apology for icons. Indeed, so long as illustrations remained decorative and symbolical, they were exempt even from attacks by the iconoclasts. François Masai points out, however, that "book illustration was practically nonexistent in western Europe during the seventh and eighth centuries" and "it may be that the victory of the iconoclasts in Byzantium is partly responsible" for the phenomenon.[8]

7. P. D'Ancona and E. Aeschlimann, *The Art of Illumination*, trans. Alison M. Brown (New York: Phaidon, 1969), p. 8.
8. François Masai, *Medieval Miniatures*, ed. L. M. J. Delaissé (New York: Harry N. Abrams, Jr., 1965), p. 12.

Whatever specific arguments exist for illustration seem to have been formulated within the illuminations and miniatures themselves and often along mutually independent lines.

Scholars have variously argued that book illustrations were used primarily for teaching purposes, and many of the illustrations are simply visual depictions of the texts. However, since most people who had access to illustrated manuscripts were able to read, there seems little reason for stressing decoration as a means for understanding the literal sense of the Bible. A general argument for its being a "poor people's Bible" in the manner that Gregory the Great had suggested for church art seems inappropriate. Nor does one have associated with books the special miracles which icons were supposed to have performed. Decoration as an act of veneration for the Word could exist, but its exact manner is uncertain. André Grabar, for example, notes that the decorations of a Byzantine liturgical roll assume that the text is the church. Accordingly, veneration of the text and its illustrations would be equivalent to the veneration of an edifice.[9] Sirarpie der Nersessian observes that the illustrations for the homilies of Gregory of Nazianzus make typological connections to the text along two separate imperialistic and theological lines. A miniature of a gospel text might suggest the crowning of an emperor or a type for Christ.[10]

In each of these areas, book illustration is only one step away from the drama. If the joining of text and images is both literal and decorative and can depict a church, the Mass, or an object of veneration, then drama would offer even

9. André Grabar, "Un Rouleau liturgique constantinopolitain et ses peintures," in *Dumbarton Oaks Papers*, no. 8 (1954), pp. 179–82.

10. Sirarpie der Nersessian, "The Illustrations of the Homilies of Gregory of Nazianzus," in *Dumbarton Oaks Papers*, no. 16 (1962), pp. 195–228.

greater possibilities of representation. As a representation, it would be historiated rather than decorative; and its images would lose none of their transcendent value in being created by a contemporary author. One of the lessons Grabar finds in the Byzantine liturgical roll is that the images retain their power despite the artist's variations. He demonstrates that "even in a learned work issued by an excellent workshop in Constantinople, one was in no way constrained to render a precise image in such conditions. This relative freedom of choice evidently did nothing to diminish the theological and symbolic value of a cycle of images in a manuscript. The liturgical text only invited the artist to choose his subject in certain iconographical categories, but it remained for the painter to choose among these subjects and consequently among a certain number of possible solutions to the iconographical problem that the theme posed." By analogy, the dramatist would have the same relative freedom in representing the transcendent and historical aspects of his work. In terms equally applicable to the playwright, Grabar speaks of an "iconographical 'zone of probability' in which the painter had to choose a subject (among several others, equally possible)."[11]

The Byzantine school of decoration which influenced the art of Montecassino was trying to moderate among different ideals. J. A. Herbert describes these styles as a "conservative ideal" of arrested action, aiming at dignity rather than energy; a "classical ideal" of beauty and the personification of abstractions like Strength and Repentance; and finally a "lively and primitive" ideal of brisk movement and action. The main purposes of the conservative ideal were theological,

11. Grabar, "Un Rouleau liturgique constantinopolitain et ses peintures," p. 186.

dogmatic, and liturgical: "profoundly anti-realistic, it pre-
ferred the solemn presentation of mysteries to the picturing
of events. It achieved its purpose by a deliberate subordina-
tion of naturalism to idea." The classical ideal strove to unite
aesthetic needs with religious instincts, and it often pressed
masterpieces of an earlier age into service as models. The
primitive ideal appears only in conjunction with the other
two styles. The representation of a martyrdom, for instance,
might contain an animated executioner going about his work
with the utmost vigor while the saint is wrapped in another
atmosphere. The frameworks incorporating these styles
might themselves be "continuous," "ornamental," or "tran-
sitional"—the last of these a state somewhere between the
animated compositions of the continuous framework and the
"stately, bejewelled, highly decorative" effects of the ornamental framework.[12]

To these ideals of decoration, Montecassino scribes add a
style of illuminated letters that was primarily Western. E. A.
Lowe notes that with the election of Frederick of Lorraine
(later Pope Stephen IX) as abbot, "a style of initial decoration comes into vogue which is manifestly of German origin."[13] Herbert also detects a Celtic element in the initials
and holds that "by the beginning of the twelfth century the
Benedictine schools of Southern Italy had already advanced
far in the evolution of a distinctive style of illumination;
founded, so far as initial-ornament is concerned, on a mixture
of Celtic, Lombardic, and Teutonic (Ottonian) elements;
and deriving the composition of its miniatures mainly from
Byzantine sources, but improving on its models by adding a

12. J. A. Herbert, *Illuminated Manuscripts* (1911; rpt. New York: Burt
Franklin, 1958), pp. 37–39.
13. E. A. Lowe, *The Beneventan Script* (Oxford: Clarendon Press, 1914),
p. 11.

largeness of manner and a warmth and richness of colouring which were afterwards among the most striking characteristics of Italian painting."[14]

The author of a medieval Passion play would not require visual models merely to write his scenes. The Gospel accounts already provide the outlines of the narrative and the language for his characters. The play's documentary style would lend an aesthetic shape to the action and assert the historical element. However, to convey the transcendent elements of the Passion, the dramatist would want to incorporate visual forms connected with the liturgy. The combination would align his work with both the timeless mystery of the redemption and the historical facts of Christ's suffering. In the East, Byzantine drama relied heavily on iconography and the so-called painters' *Guide* to construct a Passion play in the thirteenth century. August Mahr argues that the scenario of the Cyprus Passion Cycle "indicates its author was familiar with the Byzantine iconography of his day. Although, in the main, he has modeled his stage directions on his literary sources, canonical as well as apocryphal and homiletic; and although he has definitely visualized some of his scenes under the influence of miniatures and other paintings which he has before his eyes, yet there is no doubt in my mind that he must have had access to a copy of that painters' *Guide*." For the medieval artists, the *Guide* prescribes the sequence and manner of representing the events of Holy Week. Mahr points out, "That includes the locale of the scene no less than the grouping of the characters and their traditional garments and physiognomy."[15]

14. Herbert, *Illuminated Manuscripts*, pp. 167–68.
15. August Mahr, *The Cyprus Passion Cycle* (Notre Dame, Indiana: University of Notre Dame Press, 1947), pp. 105–6.

In the Montecassino Passion, the connection between drama and the visual arts is equally important. Sandro Sticca has rightly emphasized the place of contemporary Byzantine miniature and monumental art in the cultural atmosphere that produced the play. Montecassino was a center for manuscript illumination. Alphanus' poem "De Casino monte" refers to the decoration of the reconstructed basilica of St. Benedict. It particularly mentions the dazzling effects of the art work.[16] The frescoes of the church at St. Angelo in Formis, presented to Desiderius in 1072, mark an even closer approach to drama. Sticca maintains that the frescoes, "in their actual unfolding of events in a series of pictorial representations, constitute a progressive narrative, an attempt to present the Bible story as a staged drama, in a basically theatrical form."[17]

The strongest evidence for a connection between drama and art, especially miniature art, lies in the manuscript of the play itself. The manuscript leaves room for twelve miniatures. They were never executed, but one can reasonably conjecture they would have followed the patterns of contemporary miniatures. Dom Mauro Inguanez suggests the following scenes were most likely the ones to be depicted:

1. Judas' bargain
2. The false witnesses
3. Peter's denial
4. Judas' repentance
5. Christ denounced by Pilate
6. The dialogue of Pilate and his wife's servant
7. Christ denounced by Pilate

16. Text in *Patrologia Latina*, ed. J.-P. Migne (Paris, 1879), CXLVII, 1234–38. In the fourth century, Prudentius had experimented with the glosses to church art as a poetic form in the *Tituli Historiarum*.

17. Sandro Sticca, "The Literary Genesis of the Latin Passion Play," in *The Medieval Drama*, ed. Sandro Sticca (Albany: State University of New York Press, 1972), p. 48.

8. Pilate washing his hands	thorns
9. Christ scourged in the pre-	11. Christ praying for his
torium by the soldiers	crucifiers
10. Christ crowned with	12. The Crucifixion[18]

In performance, these iconic depictions appear within the play's major dramatic movements. Accordingly, one has to look for the intended iconic models within the scenes of Judas' bargain, the betrayal and arrest, Christ's arraignment before Caiaphas and Peter's denial, Judas' repentance, the trial before Pilate and Procula's dream, and Christ's suffering and crucifixion. Since the last scene is such a common topic in Christian art, it will be more useful to concentrate on the visual elements in the scenes that lead up to the play's climax. Moreover, these earlier scenes are where the play's documentary and historical interests are most evident and where the playwright would have to stress the transcendent aspects of the Passion sequence.

JUDAS' BARGAIN

Pictorial representations of the bargain between Judas and Caiaphas demonstrate a wide range of possibilities in composition. In a number of manuscripts and monuments, the priest, often accompanied by other figures, simply hands money to Judas. The Montecassino Passion calls for a scene that is highly elaborate in its psychology and technique. However, a textual problem has prevented a full understanding of the scene. In his first edition (1936), Inguanez reconstructs verse six of the play as *nostra petens lumina*, 'seeking out our distinguished person.' In the revised edition (1939), he reads the line *nostra petens limina*, 'seeking our doorway.' The lat-

18. Dom Mauro Inguanez, "Un dramma della Passione del secolo XII," in *Miscellanea Cassinese*, no. 18 (1939), pp. 13–14.

ter reading is the better of the two on several accounts. The source for the line is Virgil's description (II. 256) of the Greek fleet silently approaching Troy (*litora nota petens*, 'seeking the well-known shores'). By adapting the passage, the playwright equates Judas' betrayal with the overthrow of Troy, which medieval readers saw as a paradigm of treachery and tragedy. *Petens* also carries the meaning 'soliciting.' This sense of the word establishes Judas as an independent agent, responsible in his own degree for the events he sets in motion. The idea of his 'soliciting' is also consonant with Caiaphas' realistic view of Judas, for the high priest stresses the commercial aspects of the betrayal in contrast to Judas' inflated concern for the moral well-being of the people.

In the first edition, *lumina*, 'distinguished person' or 'glory,' would reflect a sense of self-esteem which does not figure in the play's brief sketch of the high priest. He is choleric in the interview with Christ and brutally frank in the scene of Judas' repentance, answering the admission of guilt with the question, "What is that to us?" (*Quid ad nos?*—v. 130). Yet nowhere is he excessively proud. *Limina* offers the better dramatic reading and also reveals the play's joining of medieval and classical elements. In medieval Latin *limina* acquires the expanded sense of 'ecclesia.' Rhetorically, the playwright shapes the phrase to give a visual image of its meaning: Judas' soliciting (*petens*) literally occurs within the doorway (*nostra . . . limina*). The play returns to the sense of *limina* as church when the witnesses testify to Caiaphas that Christ predicted the destruction of the temple (vv. 79–81).

It is in this descriptive sense of Judas' "soliciting in our doorway" that analogies between the language of the play and pictorial representations of the bargain scene begin to emerge. In the scene of Judas' repentance, the sixth-century

Codex Purpureus Rossanensis (fol. 8) shows a canopied architectural setting with four pillars surrounding the throne of Caiaphas. Since this manuscript, most likely with the now-missing miniatures intact, appears to have reached Calabria, a paleographical center, in the middle of the seventh century, it could easily have provided the Montecassino playwright a visual model for the scene of Judas' bargain. In the Bristol Psalter, an eleventh-century Greek manuscript now in the British Museum (Add. MS. 40731), Judas extends his hand to receive a bag of money from a bearded figure whose bench is also canopied. Caiaphas' name is inscribed, and the structure in which he sits is connected to a wall and a tower extending to the left of the miniature (fol. 68). Yet another parallel may be found on the exterior wall of the crypt at Modena Cathedral (12th–13th centuries). The sculpture shows Judas (seated to the left) extending his hand toward Caiaphas (seated center) who returns a fierce glance, while Annas (seated to the right on the same bench with Caiaphas) holds a bag of money. Stone work supplies a border for this scene; and the upper portion, which is longer than the lower border, serves as a lintel.

Two other Greek gospels offer further evidence for including an architectural setting in the bargain scene. The eleventh-century gospel in the Biblioteca Medicea Laurenziana at Florence (Plut. VI, 23) represents buildings on the right side of a miniature which shows Judas receiving the silver and addressing the chief priests and captains (fol. 156^v). A twelfth-century gospel (Paris, Bibliothèque Nationale, MS. Gr. 74, fol. 196^v) depicts Judas receiving the silver from the chief priests and the soldiers who have just left a group of buildings situated to the right. The same manuscript also depicts the meeting of the chief priests with Caiaphas; behind

Caiaphas' throne is a group of buildings with oriental turrets (fol. 52).

Any consideration of these analogies must accommodate two facts. First, the gospels provide no technical direction for executing the bargain scene; they simply say that Judas met with the priests and elders to betray Christ. So if the playwright is depending strictly on textual sources, then the line "nostra petens limina" is an amazing coincidence. Second, the architectural setting implied by the line is by no means an indispensable feature of this scene in Byzantine miniatures. The Greek Laurenziana Gospel (Plut. VI, 23) which includes buildings in one miniature of the bargain has another version of this scene (fol. 53^v, accompanying Matthew 26:21–25) in which there are no buildings. The Chludoff Psalter (Moscow, Historical Museum, MS. Gr. 129, fol. 40^v) provides another example of Judas receiving money from three figures without an architectural background. Thus the indication "nostra limina" is a revealing feature of the text, and it is probable that the inspiration of this scene in the Montecassino Passion derives from Byzantine miniatures of the Passion cycle.

Yet another detail of the bargain scene points to a pictorial model for the Montecassino playwright. The play moves directly from the plans for betrayal to the accomplished act, whereas the three synoptic gospels describe the bargain as taking place before the Last Supper. Matthew relates that Judas received the money and awaited the chance to betray Christ: "And from thenceforth he sought opportunity to betray him" (Matthew 26:16). Mark has Judas approach the high priests "Who hearing it were glad; and they promised him they would give him money. And he sought how he might conveniently betray him" (Mark 14:11). Luke re-

JUDAS' BARGAIN. British Museum, Add. MS. 40731, fol. 68.

JUDAS' BETRAYAL. Bibliothèque Nationale, Nouv. Acq. Lat. 710, eighth scene.

PETER'S DENIAL. Pierpont Morgan Library, M. 639, fol. 271ᵛ.

PETER'S DENIAL. Stuttgart Psalter, Landesbibliothek 23, fol. 49.

JUDAS' REPENTANCE. Biblioteca Medicea Laurenziana, Plut. VI, 23, fol. 57.

JUDAS' REPENT-
ANCE. Bibliothèque
Nationale, Gr.
923, fol. 314.

Medieval Idea of a Theater. Rabanus Maurus, *De universo,*
XX. 36. Archivio di Montecassino, Codex Casinensis 132, p. 489.

ports essentially the same material; Judas approaches the priests and agrees to the betrayal in return for money, but only after Satan has entered him (Luke 22: 3–6). John's version is somewhat different. There is no scene in which Judas agrees to hand over Christ for a price; rather, Christ tells Judas at the supper, "That which you do, do quickly" (John 13:27) and Judas later appears in the Garden with the soldiers and officials (John 18: 3).

The play differs significantly from these textual sources. There is no break in the action for a Last Supper scene; instead, Judas asks for soldiers immediately after he receives the money from Caiaphas:

Then let Caiaphas give the silver coins to Judas, and let Judas say to the priests:
  Hurry the deed and give me some followers who are loyal and quick.
And let Caiaphas instruct the armed men to go with Judas and let him say:
  Lead these best retainers, all heavily armed, as your comrades.
(vv. 25–30)

Several interesting parallels exist for this continued action. An eleventh-century pericope in Prague (University Library, XIV, A. 13, fol. 40) shows Judas with his left hand extended and his right hand raised. To the right of him stand four figures. The first of them hands money to Judas; behind him stands another who rests a shield on the ground, while the last figure in the group draws a sword. The miniature is surrounded by a rectangular border, and the inscription on the border identifies the scene: VENDITVR A SERVO DS VT REDIMAMVR AB IPSO. An Armenian gospel dated 1262 (Baltimore, Walters Gallery, 539, fol. 190) has a miniature accompanying Mark 14:43 which also depicts the action of the armed crowd. Christ is not represented in this miniature, but Judas leads a group of men. The group includes the priests; some of them wear headdresses and one of them leans on a staff. The helmeted soldiers carry clubs, swords, and spears.

These visual correspondences between the play and the art work prove nothing conclusive in themselves. The differences in date and provenance are somewhat larger than one would like, and they cannot be minimized. Nevertheless, the correspondences do suggest the existence of a pictorial tradition which includes Judas with the soldiers before the arrest and which could have been a model of continuous dramatic action for the Montecassino playwright. In this regard, the Armenian gospel is rather important, since this area was within the cultural orbit of Byzantium and felt the influence of compositions by Byzantine craftsmen.

THE BETRAYAL AND ARREST

The play's stage directions indicate that Christ is to pray in Gethsemane while Judas makes his bargain with Caiaphas and arranges a signal with the men given him by the high priest. "Then let Judas go to that place where Jesus is praying, just as it is written above. and let Judas say in a loud voice, bending toward him and kissing this Jesus." Since the portion of the manuscript describing the earlier action is lacking, the details of the garden scene are uncertain. It may have included the agony, the apparition of the angel, or simply prayers and rebukes to the apostles who were accompanying Christ. Beyond that, it is impossible to know whether the garden scene opens the play or continues from a scene of the Last Supper. Still, the text does give some clues about the action, and these again point to analogies in Byzantine iconography.

The stage directions are exact in defining a *mansion* called "that place where Jesus is praying." The implication is that Christ is alone, or at least isolated, as the crowd enters the garden. His isolation is necessary for the three actions of the Betrayal and Arrest: the confrontation with Judas and the kiss, the seizure by the crowd, and the flight of the disciples. The actor playing Christ requires space for the first two actions of the scene, and the disciples have to make their hasty exit. The physical separation of groups of characters in monuments and manuscript miniatures fulfills these requirements. The *Codex Purpureus Rossanensis* has this separation (fol. 4ᵛ) as does the mosaic in Sant'Apollinare Nuovo (Ravenna). An eleventh-century Greek lectionary from the church of Giorgio dei Greci (Venice) illustrates Matthew's account by depicting Christ praying alone on a small mountain on the left side of the text, while he blesses the apostles on the right side (fol. 279). The twelfth-century Greek gospel from Paris (Bibliothèque Nationale, Gr. 74, fol. 54) shows the apparition of the angel to Christ and the three sleeping apostles. There is no division between these scenes; however, their vertical placement indicates not just distance but clear separation.

The betrayal scene is a prominent feature of paleochristian funerary art. Gabriel Millet observes that "on the sarcophagi, Judas comes from the left and approaches with large steps. He finds Jesus alone or sometimes followed by an apostle. At Ravenna, one counts five of them. Peter, at the head, is going to draw the sword from the scabbard and, moreover, Judas leads behind him, at some distance, a small group of soldiers in short tunics and Jews, dressed in the long cloak. Two soldiers, stretching their arms, have seized Jesus by an end of his mantle. The first menaces him with his sword. All observe the greatest calm, except Judas who hurries." The

major action of this subdued, highly abstracted version of the
betrayal in the mosaic of Sant'Apollinare Nuovo (Ravenna)
where Christ and Judas face each other, separated from their
respective groups of apostles and soldiers, is only tentative.
"Peter . . . is going to draw the sword from the scabbard,"
and the figures betray no emotional qualities in either gesture
or expression. Millet contrasts the reserve and serenity of
Hellenistic types of the scene with the brutal realism of oriental models, such as the Chludoff Psalter, and with the emotional emphasis given in works such as the Rabula Gospels.[19]
The Montecassino Passion has greater affinities to the first of
these models, for it presents the betrayal in abstract, formalized terms. Judas, for instance, greets Christ, "Hail, teacher
of truth," and even Peter's attack on Malchus is prefaced by
the image of arrows poisoned with lies. The restraint characteristic of Hellenistic and Byzantine models appears as well
in one of the play's more notable omissions—the miraculous
events recorded in John 18:3 where the soldiers approaching
Christ are thrown to the ground repeatedly.

The Montecassino Passion combines the accounts of Matthew and John in re-creating the betrayal and arrest. In the
text Christ's first line to Judas, "O amice quid venisti" ("Why
have you come, friend?"—v. 37) is nearly identical to Matthew 26:50, "Amice, ad quid venisti"; the slight modification shows an accommodation to the trochaic scheme customary in the *versus tripartitus caudatus*. The substance of the
address to the crowd also draws upon Matthew. However,
the play reverses the order of events, staging Peter's attack
on Malchus after Christ asks why the crowd chooses to seize
him now when he has been teaching daily in the temple.

19. Gabriel Millet, *Recherches sur l'iconographie de l'Evangile* (1916; rpt.
Paris: Editions E. de Boccard, 1960), pp. 326, 330, 334.

Christ ends his speech by asking the crowd whom it seeks. Peter slices off Malchus' ear only after the crowd has replied to Christ and after Christ has asked the armed men to allow the disciples to leave.

The play moves rapidly, then, from private to public confrontation. The scene with Judas is quickly sketched by the playwright, who then introduces the crowd as a choral figure. A number of miniatures attempt to catch the private confrontation between Christ and his betrayer as an isolated event. The St. Augustine Gospels (Corpus Christi College, Cambridge, MS. 286, fol. 125, 6th–7th centuries) offer an intriguing analogy to the play. In the stage directions Christ prays in solitude, and in the miniature Christ and Judas are alone at the moment of betrayal in a scene inscribed: "iudas | ihm̄ | oscu | lotradi | dit." Francis Wormwald describes the iconography: "The scene is divided into two by a billowing hill. In the top portion Christ is kissed by Judas who comes from the right. Below four soldiers with staves fall to the ground (cf. John xviii, 6)."[20] The artist divides this scene from the public confrontation of the arrest, a subject depicted in the following miniature which bears the inscription written in the left-hand margin: "iniece | runt | manus | inihm̄." There Christ is seized by two men while on the left a figure labelled PETRUS moves forward with a sword. Below a river labelled CEDRON runs from left to right. The lectionary from Giorgio de Greci (11th century) uses the arrangement of miniatures and text to achieve this kind of formal separation. To the left of the text (Matthew 26:49 ff.) a cross-nimbed Christ receives the kiss from Judas; to the right of the text appears a group of armed soldiers; below and to the left

20. Francis Wormwald, *The Miniatures in the Gospels of St. Augustine* (Cambridge: Cambridge University Press, 1954), pl. v.

Peter slices off the ear of Malchus. A psalter (11th–12th centuries) in the Biblioteca Vallicelliana (E. 24, fol. 73ᵛ) attempts to catch the moment of transition from this private scene to the public confrontation. The two figures are isolated in the center, and the gestures of the apostles and armed soldiers show they are beginning to anticipate the next action.

The change from personal to collective address reveals another detail which links the text of the Passion play to pictorial representations of the Passion sequence. Addressing the crowd, Christ says, "Coming with lanterns, weapons, clubs, and lamps, tell me whom you seek" ("Venientes cum lanternis / armis fustibus lucernis, / dicite quem queritis"—vv. 42–45). John is the source for these lines. His gospel is the only one to include the question "whom do you seek" (18: 4,7) and to specify that the scene takes place at night. The detail of John's description of the crowd is, however, rather different from that of the play. John says, "Judas therefore having received a band of soldiers and servants from the chief priests and the Pharisees, comes to that place with lanterns and torches and weapons" (18: 3). In the Vulgate, the passage reads, "Judas ergo cum accepisset cohortem, et a pontificibus et pharisaeis ministros, venit illuc cum laternis, et facibus, et armis." The important details of the passage are *laternis* (*lanternis*), 'lanterns,' and *facibus*, 'torches.' The play does not share these details with John's gospel. For *facibus* it substitutes *lucernis*, 'lamps, oil-lamps,' and stresses the substitution by a two-syllable rhyme: *lanternis / lucernis*. The sources of the change seem to lie in the relative freedom of the visual tradition rather than in a conscious reworking of John's text.

Several miniatures contemporary with the Montecassino Passion show the full details mentioned in John. An early twelfth-century Exultet roll, written and illustrated at Fondi (Paris, Bibliothèque Nationale, Nouv. Acq. Lat. 710) reads in the eighth scene, *ut servum redimeris filium tradidisti* ('to redeem the servant you gave up the son'). The accompanying scene shows a helmeted soldier, carrying a torch, grasping Christ's left wrist. Christ raises his right hand and Judas embraces him. The crowd displays lances and halberds as well as lamps suspended from long staffs. A twelfth-century psalter from St. Swithin's Priory (British Museum, MS. Cotton Nero C. IV, fol. 21) includes lanterns and torches in the same scene; a figure to the right carries the lamp, while another figure behind Judas holds a torch in his left hand which crosses over the right. Most illustrations of the night arrest depict only torches in the hands of the crowd. The figures reproduced in Millet demonstrate this tendency. An eleventh-century Greek lectionary (Biblioteca Vaticana, Gr. 1156, fol. 194ᵛ) shows torches exclusively in a betrayal scene staged in front of a city wall with buildings extending from it to the right and left. Another Greek lectionary (Bibliothèque Nationale, Supp. Gr. 27, fol. 118ᵛ, 12th century) portrays the embrace as Christ is surrounded by men carrying torches, maces, and halberds. Similarly, two of the soldiers accompanying Judas as he embraces Christ in a miniature from a Syrian lectionary dated 1216–1220 (British Museum, Add. MS. 7170, fol. 143ᵛ) carry torches.

The features of the twelfth-century Greek gospel in Paris (Bibliothèque Nationale, Gr. 74) seem to confirm the possibility of purely iconographical inspiration. First, the miniatures illustrating the betrayal scenes in Matthew, Mark, and Luke (fols. 55, 96ᵛ, and 158ᵛ, respectively) all show men carrying torches surrounding Christ. There is no textual basis for these details, since the synoptic gospels make no mention of the scene's occurring at night. Second, in the miniature accompanying John's version of the scene (fol. 202ᵛ), where there is an explicit mention of *laternis*, only torches are pictured in the hands of the soldiers who are hurled to the ground. These two discrepancies with the textual sources are explicable only in terms of an iconographical program, and the miniaturist who executed the four versions of the scene was not illustrating texts so much as following a single model of the betrayal.

There seems to exist another iconographical program for the betrayal scene in which the crowd brings only a lantern. The fresco from the north wall of the nave from Sant'Angelo in Formis (12th–13th centuries) shows Judas embracing Christ and Peter slicing off Malchus' ear. The soldiers who accompany Judas are armed, and one of the figures carries a lantern of the same design (i.e., a lantern suspended from a long staff) that appears in the early twelfth-century Exultet roll in the Bibliothèque Nationale (Nouv. Acq. Lat. 710). Another example of the single lantern illuminating the night arrest appears in a late twelfth-century psalter from Copenhagen (Kong. Bibl. Thott, 143, 2°, fol. 14). The men with Judas carry a club, a spear, and halberds, and one of them holds a lantern. In a psalter (c. 1200) from Emmanuel College, Cambridge (III. 3.21, fol. 11ᵛ) one of the figures in the crowd carries both a club and a lantern. In his modification of the passage from John's gospel, the Montecassino playwright seems to demonstrate his iconographical rather than textual inspiration for the details of the arrest scene. He not only substitutes *lucernis* for *facibus* but also emphasizes that change in a masculine rhyme with *laternis*. The analogies in art are all contemporary with the play, and in the case of Sant'Angelo in Formis one has a fresco from a church constructed under the direction of Montecassino's Abbot Desiderius.

CHRIST BEFORE CAIAPHAS AND PETER'S DENIAL

The passages in which Christ is brought to Caiaphas and later to Pilate afford the playwright a transition between the major scenes of the Passion. Each passage includes the detail of Christ bound (vv. 71, 139), and through the interviews that follow each passage Christ's hands remain tied. The stage directions for the scene with Caiaphas read, "Then while Jesus stands bound before the priests, let two men rise up from the other armed soldiers and cry against him"; for Pilate's interview they specify, "Meanwhile let the armed men lead Jesus bound before Pilate." These transitions are a practical necessity, for the playwright must change the location of his action from the garden to Caiaphas' courtyard and later from there to Pilate's residence. They might also allow for a musical interlude between the scenes. A curious feature of the text is the fact that it makes no mention of Christ being bound. Rather, after the rebuke to Peter (vv. 58–71) the stage directions show the crowd in the process of leading Christ to Caiaphas: "Then let the armed men lead Jesus bound to the priests."

In performance the binding of Christ would occur as an incidental detail. But in the text itself, the movement is from one major scene to the next. This fragmented action, conspicuous in a text in which the playwright is particularly careful in his direction, suggests again the influence of pictorial representation. The text here is sequential rather than continuous; the playwright presents a series of discrete scenes, each with its own boundaries or frames. In so doing, he accepts the same limitations as the miniaturist or the monumental artist for whom continuous action is a formal impossibility. Sant'Apollinare Nuovo offers the same sequential action as the Montecassino Passion. The Betrayal and Arrest depicts Judas, flanked by seven soldiers, about to kiss Christ; to Christ's right stand four other apostles. The next scene shows Christ conducted by two priests and other figures. The difference between pictorial and textual sources suggests even more the playwright's dependence upon the former. Christ, bound, is led to Caiaphas in the Ravenna mosaic and in an eleventh-century lectionary (Biblioteca Vaticana, Gr. 1156, fol. 194^v). In the textual source (John 18:12), however, there is specific reference to the act of binding Christ: "Therefore the crowd, and the tribune, and the ministers of the Jews seized Jesus and bound him." By reproducing the segmented action of the pictorial analogues, the play indicates the direct use of visual materials as models.

The trial before Caiaphas contains four distinct scenes in the Montecassino Passion: (1) the testimony of the false witnesses, (2) Caiaphas questioning Christ, (3) Caiaphas rending his garment, and (4) the mocking. The playwright's literary sources provide most of the details for these scenes, although visual analogues exist for them in pictorial representations from the sixth through the twelfth centuries. For example, the image of Caiaphas rending his garment ("Look, I tear the tunic"—v. 96) appears in the St. Augustine Gospels (Corpus Christi College, Cambridge, MS. 286, fol. 125), the Gospel book of Otto III (Munich, Staatsbibliothek Clm. 4453, Cim. 58, fol. 247), and in the Laurenziana Gospel from Florence (fol. 56). Christ's prophecy about the destruction of the temple which the witnesses only report in the Montecassino Passion is presented visually in a psalter from the eleventh-twelfth centuries (Stuttgart, Landesbibliothek 23, fol. 33ᵛ) where the accusers in the trial scene to the left gesture toward the temple with a draped portal on the right.

An important correspondence between the play and the visual representations lies in the technique of simultaneous staging. The play's directions call for Peter's denial to occur during the trial scene which ends with the mocking: "While these things written above are being done and while the false witnesses are accusing Jesus before Caiaphas, let the maid cry against Peter." In addition to simultaneity, the scenes have to be acted in areas adjacent to each other, since Christ glances at Peter after the third denial in a manner reminiscent of the mosaic in the nave of Sant'Apollinare Nuovo where Christ's glance encompasses both Peter and the viewer; there Peter looks directly at Christ, and a cock is on a pedestal placed directly between the two. A tenth-century fresco on the clerestory of the church of Sebastiano al Palatino (Rome) depicts both Peter's denial (left) and Christ's interview with Caiaphas (right). Peter is seated before a brazier with two other men and the maidservant is standing. In the other arcade, separated from the denial by a pillar, Christ with a roll in hand stands before Caiaphas who is seated on a faldstool. The miniature illustrating Matthew 26:67–68 in the Laurenziana Gospel (Plut. VI, 23, fol. 56ᵛ) demonstrates the same simultaneous action. Christ, on the left with a roll in his left hand, is flanked by six men; to the right are three different scenes of Peter's denial; to the far right Peter is shown weeping.

The playwright departs from his literary sources in presenting the maidservant as the only figure who interrogates Peter. In Matthew (26:69–75) two maids and then the other figures question Peter; in Mark (14:66–72) a single woman questions him twice before the others ask about Peter's association with Christ. The visual arts, however, offer several examples of the play's focus on the maid as interrogator. At Sant'Apollinare Nuovo Peter faces the maid who stands in the draped portal of a house. A gospel from Patmos (9th–10th centuries) shows Peter seated with his right hand raised toward the maid who stands with her right hand extended toward him (Mon. Giovanni, 70, fol. 176ᵛ). Another gospel (Parma, Biblioteca Palatina, pol. 5, fol. 90), dated in the twelfth-thirteenth centuries, again depicts a woman gesturing to Peter; behind her are two doorways and a pillar; in the foreground a male figure warms himself at the fire.

These scenes can, of course, be taken as representations of the first questioning common to Matthew and Mark, rather than the completed scheme of interrogation. Yet in an illustration for the reading from Matthew 27:57–75 on Good Friday in an eleventh–twelfth century Greek lectionary (Pierpont Morgan Library, M. 639, fol. 271ᵛ), a woman extends her right hand from the window of a building, gesturing toward Peter who leans on a pedestal. The cock perched on a pillar of the building indicates that the series of three denials has been completed. The Stuttgart Psalter (Landesbibliothek 23, fol. 49. 9th–10th centuries) combines this scene with the trial. To the left Christ appears before a crowned figure seated on a bench with a footstool in front of him; in the center, Peter warms his hands at the fire within the building, while a woman, the inscription ANCILLA above her, holds an object which may be a knife; to the right, Peter weeps outside the building. A cock is on the building, and the structure carries the inscription "non cantabit hoodie [sic] donec ter me negab[is]."

The eleventh-century Prague pericope (University Library, XIV. A. 13, fol. 41) shows scenes of the trial and Peter's denial in different registers. In the top register, Christ (left) gestures to Caiaphas and holds a scroll in his left hand; Caiaphas returns a gesture to Christ; and one of the two figures behind Christ extends his right hand toward Caiaphas, as if testifying. The center register is divided into three compartments by pillars. To the left, Peter is seated as the maid gestures to him with her right hand; in the middle compartment, Peter stands as a woman in slightly different costume points to him. In the right compartment, the woman in yet another costume points to Peter's head, as he faces her with his palms turned upward; to his right, a cock is perched on a pedestal. These examples appear to confirm that the playwright draws upon a visual tradition to construct his scene of Peter's denials. His technique of simultaneous staging is found in works as early as the Ravenna mosaics, the Rossano Gospels, and the Gospels of St. Augustine. His revision of the denials to focus on the maid as the sole inquisitor has striking parallels in miniatures whose manuscripts antedate the composition of the play.

JUDAS' REPENTANCE

Two different actions occur during Peter's lamentation. The soldiers lead Christ from Caiaphas' house to Pilate's residence: "During this time let Jesus be taken from the presence of Caiaphas and let them lead him bound before Pilate." At the same time, Judas returns the money to the priests and throws it on the table before Caiaphas: "Also while Peter is lamenting, let Judas carry back the coins and throw them on a table in front of Caiaphas." After the completion of the repentance scene, the playwright underscores the simultaneity of these actions by repeating the passage recited by the soldiers leading Christ and specifying, "and Judas goes out and hangs himself. Meanwhile let the armed men lead Jesus bound before Pilate." The action of Judas returning the coins appears in the mosaic in Sant'Apollinare Nuovo where Judas faces the high priest and elders before the temple whose lintel recalls the play's earlier description "nostra limina" (v. 6). The clerestory of Sebastiano al Palatino shows Judas (his head now destroyed) returning the coins to two priests who sit beside a building. The artist here attempts to freeze sequential action, for the coins are suspended in the air as Judas turns toward a tree.

The simultaneous action of the Montecassino Passion play in this scene has analogues which extend as far back as the *Codex Purpureus Rossanensis.* The Rossano Gospels have a full page miniature (fol. 8) which depicts (top) Christ before Pilate and (below) Judas returning the coins to Caiaphas, seated in a canopied architectural setting, with Annas standing. To the right of this action Judas hangs from a tree. The same sequence of action appears in the eleventh-century Laurenziana Gospel (fol. 57). As the scenes move from left to right, Judas casts money on the ground before the priests and elders, Judas hangs himself, the soldiers present Christ to Pilate, and Barabbas is set free. This sequence of action in the visual tradition would suggest two kinds of movement to the dramatist. As one reads from left to right, an historical movement develops. Yet the simultaneity of the action sets a vertical movement against the narrative flow, and allows the viewer a more complete perspective.

Another detail of the stage directions points to the visual character of the Montecassino Passion. The Laurenziana Gospel book (fol. 57) shows Judas casting money to the ground just as he does in the miniature in the Rossano Gospels (fol. 8). In the play's repentance scene, however, he throws the coins on a table in front of Caiaphas ("let Judas carry back the coins and throw them on a table in front of Caiaphas"). Moreover, there is no mention of a table in the first scene between Judas and the priests in which he agrees to the bargain.[21] This discrepancy provides further evidence that the playwright models his scene on a specific iconographical program. A ninth-century manuscript (Paris, Bibliothèque Nationale Gr. 923, fol. 314) offers a precise example of the sequence and detail of this model. The two chief priests are seated at a table with coins piled below the outstretched hands of Judas; immediately below, Judas hangs himself. The play's inclusion of a table in this scene and its omission in the earlier episode of the bargain indicate that the author draws upon individual miniatures in constructing his drama. Furthermore his reliance on the iconic scenes and the minor inconsistencies between the depictions reflect a larger attempt to present transcendent images within the drama.

THE TRIAL BEFORE PILATE AND PROCULA'S DREAM

Sticca notes the correspondences in the trial scene between the Montecassino play and the Rossano Gospels. He proposes, "The trial before Pilate in our play is significant because it appears that its author drew on available iconographical material for dramatic effects. Specifically, he seems to have utilized the Rossano Gospels' miniatures of the trial, which are a record of a monumental and canonical *Acta Pilati.*"[22] A

21. Two priests are seated behind a table and a third places money in the hands of Judas in a psalter (11th–12th centuries) in the Biblioteca Vaticana (Gr. 1927, fol. 60).

22. Sandro Sticca, *The Latin Passion Play: Its Origin and Development* (Albany: State University of New York Press, 1970), p. 92.

further correspondence between the play and the miniatures
lies in Pilate's role as judge. In the play Pilate forcefully
asserts his judicial power, saying to Christ:

I wonder very much at your being silent and never replying to such
serious charges. Do you not wish to reply to me whom you see commanding this court and who holds you bound in chains? Do you not
know that I have the power of releasing or killing you?

(vv. 229–37)

In the Rossano Gospels, William Loerke finds ascribed to
Pilate the dominant position that he will later claim in the
play. "First among the distinctive features of these scenes is
the startling importance of Pilate, enthroned in the center
between two imperial standard-bearers. Christ stands in a
subordinate position, lower and to one side. . . . Pilate's commanding position distinguishes these miniatures from almost
all other versions of the trial in early Christian and medieval
art. Other representations of this event refuse to subordinate
the sacred defendant to his secular judge."[23] The relative
placement of figures in Christ's being subordinate to the enthroned Pilate may also relate to Christ's assertion that Pilate
has no power over him, "unless this divine power were bestowed on you from above and given from heaven" ("Nisi
desuper collata / tibi esset adque data / hec potestas celitus"
—vv. 241–43). The orientation here is vertical (*desuper*),
and Christ's speech suggests a hierarchy in which Pilate,
seated above the defendant, occupies a position literally inferior to "divine power" ("potestas celitus"). In this way the
abstract notion of heavenly power is seen against the concrete
symbol of temporal authority, and there is a vertical move-

23. William Loerke, "The Miniatures of the Trial in the Rossano Gospels,"
The Art Bulletin 43 (1961), 171.

ment from heaven to the raised tribunal chair to the standing defendant.

Loerke maintains that a distinguishing feature of the Rossano Gospels is their presentation of an actual trial in an imperial court. He contrasts the attention to such details as imperial insignia and the lawful recording of the proceeding with the abstract quality of the mosaic at Sant'Apollinare Nuovo where Christ is a tragic hero rather than a defendant. The Rossano Gospels present "no ordinary tribunal in a Roman court of law but a repeated insistence upon the imperial presence, which emphasizes beyond necessity the basic theory that every judge dispensed justice in the name of the emperor. Pilate is clearly confirmed as a legitimate officer of the government, this by the scroll in his hand; his competence as judge in this civil trial is also asserted, this by the table in the center of the miniature; but beyond this, he is established with particular force as the personal representative of the emperor, this by the imperial throne upon which he sits and by the imperial standards at either side. This tribunal declares that the trial of Christ before Pilate was an action of law before a competent authority of the Roman Empire, that it transpired in a proper court of that empire, that the judge was speaking and acting in the Emperor's stead."[24]

In church art, the scenes with Pilate's wife tend to emphasize her warning to Pilate (recorded in Matthew 27:19) rather than her dream recorded in the apocryphal *Acta Pilati*. Two frescoes, dating perhaps from the early tenth century, show her in a window as she watches Pilate wash his hands. On the west wall of the church in Qeledjlar, an attendant places his hand on the shoulder of Christ, inscribed $\overline{\text{IC}}$ $\overline{\text{XC}}$,

24. Ibid., p. 177.

who stands before Pilate. Pilate, his hands washed by an attendant holding a pitcher and a basin, is seated on a tribunal chair before the pretorium. Procula appears at the window of the building. The church at Tchaouch duplicates the hand washing and Procula's appearance at the window of the building; however, a guard with an unsheathed sword attends Christ who extends his right hand to Pilate. The same details appear in the nave of Sant'Angelo in Formis where Procula is again at the window as Pilate washes his hands attended by a servant holding a pitcher and a basin.

In this scene the Montecassino Passion duplicates the monumental evidence. After the maid has delivered her message and returned, Procula sends her offstage with the command to join the other women who are weaving (vv. 226–28). However, there is no indication that Procula leaves her *sedes* and so she observes the continuing action of the trial, including the washing of the hands, just as she does in the frescoes. An example of the demon's apparition to Procula is found in the *Hortus Deliciarum* of Herradis of Landsberg in a manuscript (Strasbourg, Bibliothèque de la Ville, fol. 143) dated in the twelfth–thirteenth centuries which was destroyed by fire in 1870. The *Hortus Deliciarum* is a compendium of medieval iconography and symbolism, and its illustration of Procula's dream shows parallels with the scene outlined in the Montecassino Passion. Procula is veiled, lying on a mattress and a decorated pillow within a draped portal; a nude demon stands by her bed and touches her shoulder. In a scene immediately to the right, Procula extends her hand to a messenger who carries cloth on a staff in exactly the image conveyed by Procula's speech in the play.

The common interpretation of this scene, based on the apocrypha, explains the appearance of the demon as an attempt to thwart divine will in its plans for redeeming man. However, the composite image of weaving provides its own comment on the trial scene. The spindle is a frequent accoutrement in depictions of the Virgin, as in the Gospel Book of Countess Matilda of Tuscany (Pierpont Morgan Library, M. 492, fol. 20) which was executed at the Benedictine monastery of San Benedetto di Polirone in the late eleventh century. Despite the demon, this symbolism lends to Procula's assertion of Christ's divinity a claim for transcendence which does not figure in the play's literary sources. Still, this image must be joined to another, for it is not Procula but the maid conveying her advice to Pilate who makes the public claim. When Procula specifically orders the maid to join the other women who are weaving, the play makes a typological connection with the theme of Christ's suffering through divine will. A thirteenth-century manuscript in the Greek Patriarchal Library at Jerusalem (Codex 5, fol. 234^v) illustrates the weaving scene among its miniatures for the Book of Job. The text accompanying the illustration is the Septuagint version of Job 38:36, "And who gave to women wisdom in weaving or skill in embroidery?" William Hatch notes that the Hebrew text for the passage is sometimes interpreted, "Who hath put wisdom in the reins, or who hath given understanding to the mind?"[25] Either interpretation would emphasize what Herbert terms the "classical ideal" of Wisdom. Thus the play incorporates in the figures of Procula and her servant a claim for the transcendence of the history it depicts.

The dramatist's use of the visual arts is both general and specific. The play depends on the belief in the transcendent

25. William Hatch, *Greek and Syrian Miniatures in Jerusalem* (Cambridge, Mass.: The Mediaeval Academy of America, 1931), p. 120.

power of images, and it incorporates features of contemporary iconographical programs. The specific influence of visual models on the Montecassino Passion is most evident in the details implied by the play's language and stage directions and in the use of techniques originating in the visual arts. In the first case, one finds that details such as the description of Judas' bargain as "nostra petens limina" and the choice of the maid as Peter's sole inquisitor develop from iconographical models which antedate the play. The play draws on visual sources in specifying the lanterns as the only source of illumination in the night seizure and in calling for a table in the scene of Judas' repentance where none is mentioned in the earlier bargain scene. The play demonstrates further affinities to the pictorial arts in its technique of fragmenting scenes into a sequence of discrete visual images. The seizure and the leading of Christ to Caiaphas provide the clearest examples of this influence. The arrest scene draws on John's gospel account for Peter's attack on Malchus, and John's is the only gospel to mention the binding of Christ specifically. Nevertheless, the play moves directly from the scene with Peter to that of the soldiers leading Christ bound, omitting a binding scene explicit in the literary source. The explanation for this shift from one set image to another is found in contemporary representations of the Passion sequence which seem not to record the actual binding of Christ.

Simultaneous staging is another device linking the play to the visual arts. It appears in the sixth-century *Codex Purpureus Rossanensis* as well as in later miniature and monumental works. As a device, simultaneous staging reconciles the limitations of visual media with a desire to represent continuous action. Kurt Weitzmann has discussed this narrative problem in early Christian art, observing that monumental artists working from miniature prototypes have the options of omitting, condensing, or conflating scenes.[26] These are the same options taken by the Montecassino playwright. Pächt states the problem of continuous narrative in other terms. "How is a picture or relief whose elements are essentially immobile, and whose world is basically stilled and silent, graphically to convey, and not only vaguely to hint at, a story that unfolds in time? A story encompasses a sequence of events, but it is more than their mere succession. It is the change and the transition from one episode to the next, in short the passing of time, which we must be made to feel if the story is to become alive in our own mind."[27]

In theory at least, this problem does not exist for the dramatist who, unlike the miniaturist or the muralist, is not obliged to select a central point of action as his focus or to represent what Weitzmann describes as "an *extended cyclic narrative* where one single episode is subdivided into several phases."[28] The limitations of medium and genre are essentially different for drama which presents continuous action as a matter of course rather than ingenuity and only by a willful imposition can arrest the flow of action. Yet throughout the play one finds that the dramatist accepts precisely those narrative limitations from which his genre frees him. Each scene of the Montecassino Passion is fragmented into discrete movements and gestures. The play repeatedly demonstrates its reliance on the fixed scene as the basic dramatic unit. Through

26. Kurt Weitzmann, "Narration in Early Christendom," *American Journal of Archaeology* 61 (1957), 88–89.

27. Pächt, *The Rise of Pictorial Narrative in Twelfth-Century England*, p. 1.

28. Weitzmann, "Narration in Early Christendom," p. 86.

these general and specific correspondences, the dramatist shows his important debt to the pictorial arts. This reliance, in turn, obliges him to recur to another established form to bridge the gaps between the iconic scenes of his work.

4. The Passion Play and the Liturgy

THE ECCLESIASTICAL art of the Middle Ages is related to both the ideology and the composition of the twelfth-century Passion drama. The iconic style of the play aligns the emergent drama with an attitude toward images and the expression of mystery that develops in the East with the Cappadocian Fathers and appears in the West with Gregory the Great. In the depiction of specific scenes from the Passion, the dramatist relies on the iconographical programs of Christian art. André Grabar proposes a comparable relation between art and another form that conveys religious mystery and also bears on the creation of the Passion drama. His study of a twelfth-century Byzantine liturgical roll emphasizes the connections between art and liturgy. The two forms complement each other in expressing the transcendent nature of worship, and in certain respects the portrayal of liturgical scenes seems to inherit the power of ritual itself. These connections establish a basis for distinguishing the separate aims of drama and liturgy and for comparing the forms. In addition, such a comparison allows one to evaluate the function of an element like music within drama and liturgy.

In the Byzantine liturgical roll, individual and group figures frame the liturgies of St. John Chrysostom and St. Basil.

The combination of these marginal figures with the text allows one to move beyond an essentially static, historiated depiction. Placed in the contexts of liturgy and its musical structure, the images lose their fixity and join with the mental flow of music into the action of worship. Grabar suggests, "the manuscript of the Mass is like the edifice where one sings it. One passes through the frontispiece to an architectural structure, just as one passes through the door of the church." The miniature portrait, which constitutes the frontispiece and commonly precedes the passage into worship and the sense of the liturgical scenes, adds an historical element to the transcendence conveyed by the images and achieved in ritual: "from the first to the last of these images, the author of the book which one reads is transformed into an author of the liturgy which one sings, and this is probably the direction which this initial part of the illustration of manuscripts followed, after its formation."[1]

The portraits of the authors, as A. M. Friend, Jr., demonstrates, would be founded on earlier connections between liturgy, the visual arts, and drama. The architectural settings in the gospel book portraits derive from the *scaenae frons* of the classical theater and the standing pose of the evangelists originates in oratorical gestures.[2] So, too, the screen or *iconostasis* which separated the laity from the liturgical action is linked with drama and the visual arts. Gregory Dix indicates "it would appear . . . that in its main features . . . this screen was originally nothing but a straightforward copy of the traditional back-scene of the Byzantine theatre with its three

1. André Grabar, "Un Rouleau liturgique constantinopolitain et ses peintures," in *Dumbarton Oaks Papers*, no. 8 (1954), p. 180.
2. A. M. Friend, Jr., "The Portraits of the Evangelists in Greek and Latin Manuscripts," in *Art Studies: Medieval Renaissance and Modern*, no. 5 (1927), pp. 115–47; no. 7 (1929), pp. 3–29.

double doors." By the sixth century the introduction of a solid screen at Constantinople converted the resemblance from that of a back-scene to something closer to a veil or the front stage curtain of the modern theater.[3]

The connections between liturgy and the traditions of representation point up an essential unity in church ritual. One must examine the nature of this unity in order to understand the complex relation of the ritual to church-drama. Liturgy exists as a transcendent structure that is apprehended through its material forms. Among modern theorists, Dom Odo Casel insists that liturgy is "not an extension of aesthetically-minded ritualism, not ostentatious pageantry" but an actualization of mystery.[4] Romano Guardini finds an element of restraint in liturgy that links the ideal to the material. Such restraint helps to avoid two significant kinds of distortion. The first would create a division in liturgy by detaching matter from essence and asserting the primacy of doctrinal or spiritual content over the direct sensuous appeal of devotion. The second would reverse these priorities to emphasize the aesthetic apprehension of liturgy so that the discrimination required to make symbols disappears. The ritual form would then comprise an arbitrary reality and negate the distance and system of reference needed to represent something beyond itself. A proper view of liturgy, Guardini holds, combines discrimination with cohesion so that, while stressing the transcendence of worship, one recognizes the validity of temporal and material forms.[5]

3. Gregory Dix, *The Shape of the Liturgy*, 2nd ed. (London: Dacre Press, 1945), p. 480.

4. Dom Odo Casel, *The Mystery of Christian Worship*, ed. Burkhard Neunheuser (Westminster, Maryland: The Newman Press, 1962), p. 27.

5. Romano Guardini, *The Spirit of the Liturgy*, trans. Ada Lane (New York: Sheed and Ward, 1935).

The Montecassino Passion

The insistence on a union of the transcendent and the temporal reflects not only a modern attitude toward worship but also an historical evolution within liturgy. Josef A. Jungmann attributes part of this evolution to an early response to Gnosticism. From its inception, Christianity distinguished itself from pagan beliefs by "no restriction to a certain locality, no temples and altars, no outward show with music and pomp, but a pure worship, rising up from the hearts of the faithful, a holy *eucharistia*." However, during the second and third centuries it had to assert the material and temporal reality of its mystery against a doctrine of salvation and revelation that assigned the creation of the material world to an inferior god and rejected the concept of incarnation.[6] Classical culture provided ready-made structures for the expression of the visible and tangible. Its impact increased after Constantine's Edict of Toleration and became particularly evident in the adaptations of architecture and prayer.[7] Grabar also traces the dependence of paleochristian art on the art of the pagan Empire.[8]

Certainly more than any other form, music represents a synthesis of the ideal and the material. For the worshipper and dramatist alike, it combines mystery with an appeal to the senses. Although the early church excluded musical instruments to concentrate on plain homophonic singing, a long history results from the connections between prayer, music, liturgy, and drama. As early as the Scriptures, song is under-

6. Josef A. Jungmann, *The Early Liturgy*, trans. Francis A. Brunner (Notre Dame, Indiana: University of Notre Dame Press, 1959), p. 114.
7. Jungmann (pp. 122–33) notes the tendency toward adapting classical forms; see also Christine Mohrmann, *Liturgical Latin: Its Origins and Character* (Washington: Catholic University of America Press, 1957), pp. 47–53, 64–70.
8. André Grabar, *Christian Iconography: A Study of Its Origins*, trans. Terry Grabar, Bollingen Series, XXXV, A. W. Mellon Lectures in the Fine Arts, X (Princeton: Princeton University Press, 1968).

stood as a form of prayer. St. Paul's famous exhortation that the faithful offer the Lord "psalms, hymns, and spiritual songs" (Colossians 3:16) is joined to the image of David dancing naked before the Lord (2 Kings 6:14) to justify a protoliturgy derived in part from contemporary Jewish practices. These categories of song fuse performance and devotion, for the whole congregation participates and sings the pieces. Philo of Alexandria's first-century treatise *On the Contemplative Life* demonstrates how important the combination is to worship. In a passage taken by Eusebius as a depiction of Pentecost in the Alexandrian Church but now thought to refer to a mystical Jewish sect, Philo describes the joining of music and movement in ritual. "About halfway through the feast all rise, and first of all two choirs are formed, one of men, the other of women. As leader and conductor of each, the most honourable and suitable is chosen. Then they sing hymns in honor of the deity in various metres and tunes, sometimes in unison, sometimes antiphonally in well-ordered melodies, gesticulating and dancing as if in ecstasy: now processional, now stationary hymns, executing strophe and antistrophe in choral dance." This observance follows typological lines in recalling the crossing of the Red Sea and identifying the leaders as Moses and Miriam. Philo specifically defines the effect and intention of the songs and movements: "they make harmonized and very melodious music. Very beautiful are the conceptions, beautiful the words, and noble the performers. And the object alike of the conception, words, and performers, is reverence."[9]

The effects and intentions of liturgical song can also be realized apart from the external actions of worship. The flow

9. Quoted in Egon Wellesz, *Eastern Elements in Western Chant* (Copenhagen: Munksgaard, 1947), p. 52.

of music within the worshipper himself can achieve similar results. In the passage from the *Confessions* (IX, 6) that records his baptism, St. Augustine mentions the effects of the singing in St. Ambrose's Milanese Church, whose music some historians trace through Byzantine sources to a Near Eastern origin. Augustine recalls, "The tears flowed from me when I heard your hymns and canticles, for the sweet singing of your Church moved me deeply. The music surged in my ears, truth seeped into my heart, and my feelings of devotion overflowed, so that the tears streamed down. But they were tears of gladness." Later at the death of his mother, Augustine returns to the influences of music and comforts himself by remembering the verses of Ambrose's hymn "Deus, Creator omnium" (IX, 12).[10]

Augustine's successors inherited a theory of music from classical Antiquity through writers like Boethius and Martianus Capella.[11] The theory emphasized music as a *speculum* or mirror of the universal order. It divided music hierarchically into three kinds: *in instrumentis constitua*, *musica humana*, and *musica mundana*. By a sympathetic movement based on numbers, man would be tied to a reaction which, in the first case, is to the harmony of sounds; in the second, to the harmony of relationships like body and soul; and in the third, the *musica mundana*, to a harmony with the entire universe. As liturgy and drama incorporate music in their structures, they do so as a possible means of emphasizing transcendence through numbers and rational order. Just as the tripart division of language into literal, typal, and moral levels

10. St. Augustine, *Confessions*, trans. R. S. Pine-Coffin (Baltimore: Penguin Books, 1961), pp. 190, 202.

11. Egon Wellesz, "The Survival of Greek Musical Theory," in *A History of Byzantine Music and Hymnography*, 2nd ed. (Oxford: Clarendon Press, 1961), pp. 46–77.

would aim toward a moral sense in medieval religious writing, so, too, religious music aims toward its moral equivalent —the music of the spheres. In both liturgy and drama, the rhythm of this movement is determined by syntax. The lack of a sophisticated system of notation in early medieval music compels the musical form to follow the same *ictus* of the words that unscored speech would demand.

The later adoption of responsory and antiphonal singing creates different structures that affect the form and action of liturgy and church-drama, but it does not modify the theoretical aspects of music. Responsory singing divides the community by establishing social roles within prayer. The precantor directs the song, just as the chorus leader directs the chorus in archaic classical drama. The repetition of the musical segments links the different roles of precantor and choir. E. Catherine Dunn finds a structure approximating drama in the patterns of repetition. She maintains, "responsorial singing constitutes a much closer approach to dialogue than the antiphonal because the division of parts often involves 'address' to the whole choir by their precantor"; in the lessons connected with the singing "the lector himself has been addressing the group of his fellow choristers through a quoted voice."[12]

References to antiphonal singing appear as early as Pindar's fragments, and they indicate a performance in which high voices respond to deep voices with the same melody. In the fourth century, the practice was adopted by monastic communities in the Antioch Church. Antiphonal singing proceeds by dividing the chorus into semi-choruses and apportioning

12. E. Catherine Dunn, "Voice Structure in the Liturgical Drama: Sepet Reconsidered," in *Medieval English Drama: Essays Critical and Contextual*, eds. Jerome Taylor and Alan H. Nelson, Patterns in Literary Criticism, 11 (Chicago: The University of Chicago Press, 1972), pp. 49, 50.

alternate verses to them. These divisions often assume the patterns of dialogue, and scholars have observed the formal correspondences between the antiphonal framework of pieces like the *quem queritis* trope and the exchanges between characters in drama. Rosemary Woolf points out these correspondences may be fortuitous. "Choirs sang the psalms and other pieces antiphonally and therefore when two adjoining verses consisted of question and answer they might momentarily seem to be engaged in dialogue."[13] Nonetheless, Guardini stresses the role of dialogue in making the interior needs of worship visible. The antiphonal singing would divide "those present into two choirs, and cause prayer to progress by means of dialogue." It would also create a leader "to regulate the beginning, omissions, and end, and, in addition, to organize the external procedure" according to a model of interior needs.[14]

The ability of song to combine external symbols with interior needs conveys something of the transcendent power of music. In the Pythagorean and Neoplatonic idea of a *musica mundana*, song is continuous; and without diminishing its power men periodically articulate the song. In legend poets like Romanos or Caedmon receive divine inspiration for their songs through visions, but most men understand the one song as many. They sense the discontinuities that arise between acts of celebrations. However, by a kind of metonymy, music allows for referential gestures that recall a total structure. In the same way, an introductory phrase may recall the entire melody and context for a piece of liturgical music. As a transcendent structure, liturgy shares many features of this dual

13. Rosemary Woolf, *The English Mystery Plays* (Berkeley and Los Angeles: University of California Press, 1972), p. 5.
14. Guardini, *The Spirit of the Liturgy*, pp. 135–36.

nature. It is at once an autonomous form and a social reality with collective rather than personal intent. It exists outside time, encompassing and entering history; and its historical enactment abolishes the distance between the human and the divine.

The transcendent nature ascribed to liturgy and medieval music provides an important contrast for examining the relation of liturgy to drama and particularly to the Passion drama. Like liturgy, the church-drama deals with the transcendent through its material forms. It uses the same devices of visual art and images, gestures, and costumes to assert the reality of Christian mystery. The incorporation of music can provide a total framework for dramatic action or a series of interludes between the episodes. These interludes would establish boundaries around scenes, renew focus on the action, allow the illusion of time's passage, or provide bridges between the scenes. Either as a total framework or as an interlude, music brings a vertical, sympathetic movement to offset the historical, empathetic movement of dramatic action. But in contrast to liturgy, early church-drama would not intend to evoke the whole of salvation history. A drama that concerns the Passion means to concentrate on one element and not to capitulate Christian time.

The emergence of church-drama as a supplement to what is theoretically an all-embracing form presents problems in itself. It suggests changes have occurred in either the psychological needs of the worshippers or the structure of liturgy. Both kinds of change would create impressions of lack. In the first case, the lack would result from the worshippers' making demands that the form had not been equipped previously to satisfy. In the second case, the lack would result from removing or altering something that the worshippers

had come to expect; their expectations would have to be fulfilled another way. Carl Jung uses these terms to propose that
a gradual distancing of Christ's humanity accounts for the
origins of Mariolatry in the need of Christians to have a human mediator.[15] In liturgy Christ may have eventually become so divorced that more human representations were
needed. The allegories devised for the Mass by Amalarius
of Metz and Honorius of Autun reflect a need to reestablish
an historical element in liturgical mystery. In this respect, one
can see the Passion drama offering an alternative to the symbolic nature of liturgy and to liturgy's shunning of naturalism
to present supernatural facts *in mysterio*. As H. A. Reinhold
points out, a Passion play insists on a histrionic level, whereas
liturgy offers not a mimetic crucifixion but a genuine reenactment through readings, lamentations, prayers, and divinely
instituted Eucharist.[16]

Historians of the liturgy are careful to distinguish two
forms: the Mass and the divine offices. By the twelfth century, each had undergone a long development along often
distinct lines. Anton Baumstark uses the term "Cathedral
Rite" for the first and "Monastic Rite" for the second. Either
form would be, as Dix proposes, "the act of taking part in
the solemn corporate worship of God by the 'priestly' society
of christians, who are 'the Body of Christ, the church.' " He
further specifies that the act of worship presupposes the eucharist.[17] In the early formations of liturgy, when the church
was assimilating converts and diverse religious practices, the

15. Carl Jung, *Mysterium Coniunctionis*, trans. R. F. C. Hull, 2nd ed., in
The Collected Works of C. G. Jung (Princeton: Princeton University Press,
1970), XIV, 176.
16. H. A. Reinhold, *Liturgy and Art* (New York: Harper and Row, 1966),
pp. 52–56, 61, 95.
17. Dix, *The Shape of the Liturgy*, p. 1.

nature of the form was syncretic. Baumstark points out that new elements were added to the old until gradually a satisfactory revised form was achieved. He proposes liturgical development includes periods in which "primitive elements are not immediately replaced by completely new ones, the newcomers at first take their place alongside the others."[18]

By the fourth century this revised form followed the general sequence of an introduction (*synaxis*, 'meeting') and a spiritual sacrifice (*eucharistia*). The *synaxis* consisted of readings, songs, homilies, and prayer; and it was easily adapted from the worship of the synagogue. "To the books of the Jewish Bible," Léopold Duchesne explains, "were soon joined, in the lector's pulpit, the writings of the New Testament, among which a special emphasis was given to the Gospel. These were all the changes, except of course those which the new orientation given to faith introduced in the text of the prayers and homilies as well as in the choice of Biblical lessons and sacred songs."[19] In this scheme, the *synaxis* gives a prominence to language and diction which continues the oratorical character historians observe in church liturgies, above all in the Roman rite. The emphasis on readings affords a sense of continuity between the Old and New Laws in the texts and in the character of the worship. This continuity depends in turn on a notion of fulfillment. Christ is presumed to change the nature of liturgical language from prophecy and the evocation of God to a celebration of redemption. Therein, the liturgy postulates an achieved history that encompasses all time.

Texts of the eucharistic prayer date from as early as Hippol-

18. Anton Baumstark, *Comparative Liturgy*, trans. F. L. Cross (London: A. R. Mowbray and Co., 1958), p. 23.
19. Léopold Duchesne, *Origines du culte chrétien*, 5th ed. (Paris: Editions E. de Boccard, 1925), p. 49.

ytus of Rome's *Apostolic Tradition* of the third century.
Jungmann characterizes the prayer preserved in Hippolytus
as "essentially a prayer of thanksgiving, an *eucharistia*," and
he argues for its autonomy. "This is the only prayer of the
Mass proper—what we would call the canon. In fact, it is the
only prayer said at the service, for no Fore-Mass ordinarily
precedes," although prayer services and instruction could occur earlier in the day. The autonomy of the prayer is conveyed
by its form, which is a life of Christ. The prayer recounts the
Incarnation, Passion, Resurrection, and repeats the words of
institution at the Last Supper. To these transcendent events,
it adds a temporal, empathetic dimension by commanding
repeated expressions of thanksgiving from the congregation.
In the Latin translation made of Hippolytus, the prayer opens
with thanksgiving and mention of the Incarnation and Passion. "We offer thanks to you, God, through your chosen son
Jesus Christ whom you sent to us in the earliest times as savior,
redeemer, and angel of your will. He is your inseparable
word through whom you made everything and it was pleasing to you. You sent him from heaven into the virgin mother;
remaining in her womb, he was made flesh and the son was
shown to you born from the holy spirit and the virgin. Fulfilling your will and gaining the holy people for you, he
spread his hands when he suffered so that he might free
those who believed in you."[20]

The liturgy known to the twelfth-century Passion dramatist had advanced beyond the eucharistic prayer of Hippolytus, but it had also reversed the tendency toward syncretism.
A century before the play, within a year of his election as
pope in 1057, Stephen IX suppressed the earlier Ambrosian

20. Jungmann, *The Early Liturgy*, p. 67.

chant at Montecassino where he had been a monk and later abbot. The suppression was part of a new centralization of liturgy that occurred during the mid-eleventh century when a number of German prelates assumed posts in the major dioceses of Italy and brought liturgical books with Roman Ordines. The Ordines themselves had been adapted to local traditions during the Carolingian renaissance of the ninth century. The titles of many Ordines suggested a tie with early Roman ecclesiastical practices, in keeping with Charlemagne's order, "Return to the fountain of St. Gregory."[21] At Montecassino, as Teodoro Leuterman notes in his study of the twelfth-century liturgy, among clear preservations of older and Oriental practices, the German influence appears in the adoption of hymns like "Ubi caritas et amor" from the Gallican rite as substitutes for those prescribed in Gregory the Great's Roman Ordines.[22]

The movement toward centralizing liturgical practices has a counterpart in contemporary musical practice. Music historians draw attention to the eleventh century as an era when standardization becomes more evident. Improvisation gives way to composition, and musical notation develops to the point where a piece can be written in a fixed form. The musical notation for a *planctus* in the manuscript of the Passion play shows the effect of this last development. In a recent survey of research, Marilynn Smiley notes that the principal Western theorists of the century are connected with Benedictine monasteries. She observes in their work an increasing

---

21. S. J. P. Van Dijk and J. Hazelden Walker, *The Origins of the Modern Roman Liturgy* (Westminster, Maryland: The Newman Press, 1960), pp. 69–70.

22. Teodoro Leuterman, *Ordo Casinensis Hebdomadae Maioris (saec. xii)*, in *Miscellanea Cassinese*, no. 20 (1941), p. 57. Hereafter cited as *Ordo*.

emphasis on the practice of music, a concern with organum, and a stress on the place of music within liturgy.[23] One of the most important compilations of these theories and practices is an eleventh-century Cassinese manuscript, Codex Casinensis 318. It contains works by Guido of Arezzo, Odo (from the Abbey of Saint-Maur des Fossés), Hucbald, and Johannes Presbyter.

The centralization in liturgy and music would have some impact on the creation of a Passion drama. For the liturgy especially, it removes the possibility of modifications to fit new or local needs. A liturgy capable of adapting itself to those needs would not have to devise extra-liturgical means for expression. Conversely, a centralized, "reactionary" liturgy would make the new observances necessary. The changes apparent in the twelfth-century Montecassino Ordo imply the need there for local adaptations. In this respect, a Passion drama would satisfy needs in a way authorized ritual could no longer support. The nature of the already accepted Passiontide observances would also create special conditions for later innovations in liturgical practice. Such commemorative rituals as the blessing of the palms, the Adoration of the Cross on Good Friday, and the lighting of the Paschal candle at the Easter vigil derive their authority from ecclesiastical practice rather than Scripture. As a result, some innovations can be made without affecting doctrine or mystery; in fact, such innovations can have a consciously historical character. Baumstark maintains that there is for the commemorative ceremonies "the radiating influence of a very definite ecclesiastical centre, which will almost always be the ancient Chris-

23. Marilynn Smiley, "Eleventh Century Music Theorists," in *ACTA: The Eleventh Century*, eds. Stanley Ferber and Sandro Sticca (State University of New York at Binghamton: The Center for Medieval and Early Renaissance Studies, 1974), pp. 83, 61–64.

tian Jerusalem."[24] In assuming the context of these observances, the Passion drama would align itself more with the
traditions of ecclesiastical practice than with the Mass and
the cultic expressions of mystery. Thus, it will be useful to
consider the form of worship in Monastic Rite and then to
examine the first Passion play in the context of Montecassino's
ceremonies for Good Friday.

An important element of Monastic Rite is its emphasis on
continuity. For the primitive church, the celebration of the
eucharist represented an active denial of pagan daily life.
Rather than live in unconnected time, the church chose to
center on its faith by adopting a scheme of daily private devotions from Hebrew practice. Hippolytus outlines the time
of the devotions as midnight, cock-crow, the third, sixth, and
ninth hours, and the evening. Yet not until the ascetic and
monastic movements of the fourth century were these private
devotions communal. They became so under a general redi-
rection of the church toward sanctifying human life and time.
"The church at large," Dix maintains, "just because she was
in the world, could not renounce all secular life as the monk
did, but she learned from him to sanctify it." The private devotions emerge as daily offices first in Antioch and, in the age
of Egeria's *Peregrinatio*, soon afterwards at Jerusalem under
the direction of St. Cyril. Around 382 Pope Damascus "deliberately modelled the Roman office in its main lines on that
of Jerusalem."[25] The proliferation and elaboration of the
offices at other ecclesiastical centers and basilicas owe much
to the affluence and leisure from ordinary activity which the
monastic movement afforded. Its support came not only from
the people at large but also from the circles around the im-

24. Baumstark, *Comparative Liturgy*, p. 140.
25. Dix, *The Shape of the Liturgy*, pp. 320, 329.

perial court through conversions such as the one Ponticianus recounts in Augustine's *Confessions* (VIII, 6).

In the monastic restructuring of time, the purpose of dividing the day is to direct the mind at crucial junctures toward God through mental rather than eucharistic activity. The hours of Terce, Sext, and Nones, for instance, recall the hours of the Passion. Liturgical drama, as historians of the form have shown, develops in part out of these and other additions to the authorized liturgy in monastic practice. At Montecassino, as in other Western monasteries, the offices follow the patterns of the *Ordines Romani*, which often derive from Oriental usage, as well as the observances set down in St. Benedict's *Regula Monachorum*. The Rule in fact anticipates the Roman practices of the twelfth century by allowing hymns to be added to the scheme of psalms, antiphons, responses, and prayers in the office. The Monastic Rite was affected in turn by Eastern elements that are apparent in both the Paschal vigil and the addition of the Adoratio crucis to the offices sung on Good Friday.

In his study of the Holy Week Ordo, Leuterman confirms Jerusalem as the second major influence, after Rome, on the rituals of Montecassino. The influence is part of an overall "gradual infiltration of the Greek liturgy into the Latin rite."[26] The early churches of Rome and Alexandria did not celebrate the eucharist even in the ordinary week, and the Western church continued what was considered a "tone of mourning" for Good Friday. Historically, the tone of mourning in the services may have been accidental. "In reality," Jungmann says, "these practices were not introduced to give the services the character of mourning; they are very ancient practices preserved from a time when the liturgy was

26. *Ordo*, p. 57.

still very simple." The Mass was suspended, and the service consisted of readings and closed with solemn prayers. "For the rest, the day was passed in silent mourning as a day of penance."[27] Leuterman also draws attention to the tone for the day. "In the first centuries the Mass was not celebrated on this day, because it was considered a day of sadness, while the Mass always indicates a spiritual joy."[28] As an avenue of development, the tone of mourning has given rise to the now disputed view that the origin of the Passion play is in the *planctus*.

In contrast to Western practices, the Byzantine rite focuses more on the deliverance through the crucifixion and allows its observances to be elaborate and celebratory. This optimistic tone fosters a different kind of liturgy to join with a music that Egon Wellesz finds of "a markedly dramatic character." "Melody and words," he argues, "aim at a strong accentuation of expression."[29] The optimistic tone also permits the introduction of dramatic elements into the offices for the special feasts. Liutprand, bishop of Cremona, visited Constantinople in 968 and told of seeing a celebration of a translation of Elijah *in ludis scenicis*. The context of the remark is vague, but he seems to express shock at either finding the Hagia Sophia turned into a theater or seeing pagan plays on saints' days. Conversely, a Greek who attended the seventeenth Council was shocked to see a play on the Passion being performed *outside* the church in Florence in the fifteenth century.[30] Giorgio La Piana finds such an accommodation of drama to liturgy in the nature of Byzantine ritual. "Alternate

27. Jungmann, *The Early Liturgy*, p. 262.
28. *Ordo*, p. 67.
29. Wellesz, *Eastern Elements in Western Chant*, p. 120.
30. Marjorie Carpenter, *The Kontakia of Romanos, Byzantine Melodist* (Columbia, Missouri: University of Missouri Press, 1970), I, xxii.

recitations and singing of psalms and anthems, litanies, acclamations, hymns with solo and choirs, not to speak of the use of profane melodies and ceremonies denounced as abuses by rigid moralists and ascetic monks, had given to the Byzantine liturgy such a spectacular character that the introduction of recitation of dialogues by many would fit well into the picture."[31] On Good Friday dramatic sermons like the kontakia focus on the denial of Peter, Mary at the Cross, and the Passion. Yet even here the incidents are viewed in terms of celebration, for they are joined by a kontakion on the Victory of the Cross.

Montecassino, which appropriated from both the Eastern and Western rites, made available to its dramatist the choice of either the tone of mourning prevalent in the West or the optimistic attitude of the East. On Good Friday both traditions abandon the Mass and adopt a monastic liturgy. The offices for the day constitute a *synaxis*, and the drama would depict the sacrifice that the Mass presents *in mysterio*. Thus the liturgical context of the play would seem to extend to the twelfth century O. B. Hardison, Jr.'s, thesis that "ritual *was* the drama of the early Middle Ages," and that ceremonies like the Easter Vespers of the Gregorian age provide more than a simple environment for drama.[32] At the same time, however, the combination of the offices and the play at Montecassino reflects the fundamental differences between the drama and liturgy. Although the play deals with the Crucifixion, it contains neither the thanksgiving of the primi-

31. Giorgio La Piana, "The Byzantine Theater," *Speculum* 11 (1936), 178.
32. O. B. Hardison, Jr., *Christian Rite and Christian Drama in the Middle Ages: Essays in the Origin and Early History of Modern Drama* (Baltimore: The Johns Hopkins Press, 1965), p. 123; "Gregorian Easter Vespers and Early Liturgical Drama," in *The Medieval Drama and Its Claudelian Revival*, eds. E. Catherine Dunn, Tatiana Fotitch, and Bernard M. Peebles (Washington: Catholic University of America Press, 1970), pp. 27–40.

tive eucharistic prayer nor the sacramental mystery of the Mass. The action it represents is transcendent, but the form of drama remains historical. The playwright is not seeking to add new elements to ritual; rather, he is seeking to establish recognition of his own intentions.

The Good Friday liturgy is especially suited to being adapted to new religious purposes. The character of the feast day requires a thematic cohesion in the offices that exceeds the unity of even the proper readings for a Mass. Although prayers and song alternate with readings and ritual actions, they all concentrate on the events of the Passion. In these different aspects of commemoration, the offices also encompass the ecclesiastical traditions of the East and West. They express both mourning and celebration but do so in a discursive manner based on thematic repetition rather than dramatic action. Whereas the offices are shaped along the lines of musical composition and repetition, the action of the play is shaped by the gospels and the form of legal process. A close study of the Holy Week Ordo will indicate the differing procedures of the Good Friday liturgy and the Passion play.

Although the Ordo shows that Montecassino in the twelfth century had progressed beyond the readings in a *synaxis* of Hosea, Exodus, and John, the added psalms and antiphons of the nocturns of Holy Week still retain a focus. Externally they evoke a Passion narrative along the lines of recall. In the first nocturn, each psalm prefigures an event of the Passion sequence. The plot against Christ is anticipated in the verse "the rulers take counsel together, against the Lord, and against His Christ" (Psalm 2:2) and Psalm 21 describes the action of sacrifice as an evocation of the Crucifixion. Augustine's *Enarrationes in psalmos* is one of the texts for the second vigil. By explaining that the passages from the psalms are not only psalms but also foreshadowings of actual events in the Passion, it establishes the reverberatory nature of the office. *"Why do the heathen rage, and the people meditate vain things? The Kings of the earth have stood up and the rulers taken counsel together, against the Lord, and against His Christ*. It is said, *why?* as if it were said, in vain. For what they wished, namely Christ's destruction, they accomplished not; for this is spoken of our Lord's persecutors, of whom also mention is made in the Acts of the Apostles" (4:26).[33] The verses dealing with sacrifice similarly prefigure the Passion: *"Many calves came about Me; fat bulls closed Me in*. The people, and their leaders: the people, *many calves*; the leaders, *fat bulls. They opened their mouth upon Me, as a ravening and roaring lion*. Let us hearken to their roaring in the Gospel, *Crucify, Crucify*" (John 19:6). In *Enarratio II* for Psalm 21, Augustine reveals further correspondences between the psalm and the Passion and emphasizes the need to remove enigmas from Christian history. "What God would not have passed over in silence in His Scripture," he says, "must not either by us be passed over in silence, and by you must be heard. The Lord's Passion, as we know, happened once: for once hath Christ died, the Just for the unjust" (1 Peter 3:18).

The typology and symbolism that theorists like Guardini see at work in liturgy are evident in the nocturns where the voice of David strengthens the figural evocation of the Passion. Coeval with the typology of David and Christ on an abstract level is a movement toward the Passion on a literal

33. All translations of Augustine's *Enarrationes in psalmos* are those of *Expositions of The Book of Psalms of S. Augustine, Bishop of Hippo* (London: F. and J. Rivington, 1847).

142

level to assert both the promise and actuality of Christian mystery. The counterpointing verses and responsories of Matins shape a narrative around different incidents of the Passion sequence. In the first nocturn, Augustine's theme of the just suffering for the unjust is amplified through the figures of Barabbas and the two thieves. "*Responsory*: The veil of the temple has been torn, and all the earth trembled; the thief cried from the cross, saying: Remember me, Lord, when you come to your kingdom. *Verse*: I say to you, today you shall be with me in Paradise. *Verse*: The thief said to the other thief: We are worthy of receiving this punishment, but what did this one do? Remember." In the third nocturn, Barabbas merges with Judas, and the chorus repeats Christ's words. "*Responsory*: The thief Barabbas is set free and the innocent Christ is killed; for Judas, led on by the crime, who overturns peace to make war, betrayed the Lord Jesus Christ with a kiss. *Verse*: The truth is given to the liars, the impious whip the pious. You come to lay hold of me with swords as you come for a thief. Daily I was among you, teaching in the temple, and you did not seize me."

All these incidents carry over into the Passion play and reveal there an important difference of the office from drama. Because of its musical basis, the Good Friday office can evoke the Passion without imitating the narrative sequence of Scripture. The evocations also have aims distinct from those of drama. In drama, they tend to recall the literal, but in the offices the evocations serve as an overture to the action of ritual and allow one to organize responses to mystery. Hardison traces the development of these responses in Cathedral Rite and notes that even before Passiontide, "the tension between these two opposing themes is . . . expressed, most directly in the imagery of agon. References to warfare, armor, and various kinds of struggle recur in the liturgy. At first the agon is generalized; that is, it is projected as a conflict between two factions best identified as 'the forces of darkness' and 'the forces of light,' rather than as a specific antagonist and protagonist." He goes on to say, "As Passion Sunday approaches, a sharpening of dramatic focus is evident. Two groups are isolated from the body of the congregation. The alienation theme attaches to the penitents, who are expelled from the church as Adam from the original Paradise, while the redemption theme is centered on the *electi*, who are formally labeled 'Christian soldiers' as they receive the Creed. The *electi* are not, however, entirely pure. If they are Christian soldiers, they are also in a real sense the battleground for the war between the forces of darkness and light."[34]

A comparable tension occurs in the monastic offices and the play. This tension has in part to do with the tone of mourning which the Western tradition imposes on the Passion. In the first nocturn, David asks, "My God, my God, why have you forsaken me?" (Psalm 21:1) and implores, "But you, O Lord, be not far from me" (Psalm 21:20). In the psalm immediately following, however, he adopts another attitude which permits him to call God "my light and my salvation" (Psalm 26:1) and recall, "he will set me high upon a rock. Even now my head is held high above my enemies on every side" (26:6). This alternation between alienation and spiritual unity is resolved temporarily in the vigil. The essentially positive tone of Psalm 2, on which it begins, asserts a unity between man and God that makes possible a celebration of the spiritual sacrifice. The antiphon "Vim faciebant" from the second nocturn amplifies the theme of alienation. Whereas

34. Hardison, *Christian Rite and Christian Drama in the Middle Ages*, p. 109.

earlier the speaker could say, "Many dogs surround me; the council of evil encircled me" and "Liars surrounded me; without cause they fell on me with whips," now the speaker turns attention to his interior being. He says, "There is no health in my flesh because of your indignation; there is no wholeness in my bones, because of my sin" (Psalm 37:4). Later, in the play, Peter will respond to a similar awareness of himself with the admission, "Oh, how deeply I have sinned."

The other psalms read at the second nocturn continue these themes of alienation and redemption. In Psalm 39 the speaker again sees himself threatened by external forces; however, his relation to God has changed. The alienation is dissipated, and he can ask, "Let all be put to shame and confusion who seek to snatch away my life. / Let them be turned back in disgrace who desire my ruin" (15–16). In Psalm 53 the prayer is "Turn back the evil upon my foes; in your faithfulness destroy them" (7). Within the office, readings from Augustine's *Enarratio in psalmum LXIII* provide an explanation for the external threats reiterated in the first two vigils. These threats are concentrated in the verse "Hear, Lord, my prayer, while I am troubled; from the fear of the enemy deliver my soul," and Augustine asserts there that the purpose of external threats is to test faith. The prayer is not for deliverance from death, he points out, but for deliverance from the fear of death. "Therefore for this prayeth the voice of the Martyrs, *From fear of the enemy deliver Thou my soul*: not so that the enemy may not slay me, but that I may not fear an enemy slaying." "From fear of the enemy deliver my soul," he paraphrases, "I would not fear him that hath killeth the body, but I would fear Him that hath power to kill both body and soul in the hell of fire. For not from fear would I be free:

but from fear of the enemy being free, under fear of the Lord a servant." This moral distinction reappears in the action of the Passion play. The priests and Caiaphas' men replace the enemies who menace David. The trial of faith which Augustine sees in the threat of the "enemy slaying" assumes dramatic form at the seizure, and the disciples who flee individually fail precisely those conditions which Augustine sets out.

The psalms of the third nocturn of Matins develop within these poles of alienation and redemption. In Psalm 58 David again sees external threats, and a social estrangement objectifies the spiritual isolation behind his pleas: "Rescue me from my enemies, O my God; from my adversaries defend me. / Rescue me from evildoers; from blood-thirsty men save me. / For behold, they lie in wait for my life; mighty men come together against me" (2–4). In Psalm 87 divine wrath is viewed as the cause of the alienation: "Upon me your wrath lies heavy, and with all your billows you overwhelm me. / You have taken my friends away from me; you have made me an abomination to them" (8–9) and "Companion and neighbor you have taken away from me; my only friend is darkness" (19). Yet in Psalm 93 the structure of alienation is reversed, and the office begins to assert the possibility of redemption. The speaker remains a solitary figure, but God is here his ally: "Who will rise up for me against the wicked? Who will stand by me against evildoers?" (16). The Passion play's handling of these themes carries out the sense of the typology. The alienation expressed verbally by Peter in his denial of Christ and visually by his physical isolation from the other disciples is substantially the same as that expressed in Psalm 87. Yet the form of the drama and its visual character permit an even greater elaboration of the theme. For Peter the disciples are a collective mirror of his individual rejection of Christ, and the point is made dramatically when he rejoins them. Christ's isolation in the trial scene with Pilate restates David's question, "Who will stand by me against evildoers?" In these connections, the playwright treats the lyricist's metaphors as dramatic images and uses them not only to echo the Good Friday office but also to set up an aesthetic balance within his own work.

After Lauds and the recital of the Kyrie on Good Friday, the community begins to sing the psalter in a manner which incorporates ritual action. The Ordo prescribes that "these verses [of the Kyrie] being finished, let them begin to sing the Psalter barefoot in the choir." Leuterman proposes that the exercise of remaining barefoot is a guide to the tone of the office and "was a special form of penance which aimed to recall in a practical manner the sufferings and Passion of Our Lord and which at Montecassino with its stone floor and still cold temperature of the season made it certainly more accentuated."[35] This act of penance engages the community in the expanded sense of involvement which will be intensified in the reading of the martyrology, the gestures accompanying the Passion gospel, and the Adoratio crucis. The psalms which up to this point had merely recalled and taught, now make active what has been recalled. The offices become mimetic as the individual assents to the suffering. In a penance designed to indicate parallels with the Crucifixion, the liturgy moves from a meditative and devotional service to an external action. The offices thus concentrate the large harmonic pattern of Christian devotion in a single imitable act, much as the eucharistic prayer of the early church had joined transcendent events to an expression of thanksgiving.

Prime occurs during the singing of the psalter, and the

35. *Ordo*, p. 52.

readings and the antiphon of the hour amplify the themes of devotional exercise. The antiphon, "The thief cried from the cross, saying: Remember me, Lord, when you come to your kingdom," focuses on redemption; but at the beginning of Prime, Psalm 21 is again recited. Leuterman attaches a special significance to the repetition of the psalm. "To judge from the documents, this usage was the Cassinesi's own, and is also another proof of the profound liturgical significance of the day in question, because this psalm is adapted in a truly special way to the desolation, suffering, and Passion of our Lord."[36] Thus, at the imagined center, the enactment of suffering and the recitation of the psalter are structured to commemorate the Passion. The alienation stressed in the psalm is set against the redemption promised by the antiphon in a context that not only preserves the dual Eastern and Western traditions on which the Cassinese Ordo was based but does so in a way that intensifies the dramatic elements in the office.

Following the recitation of the psalter, the office introduces actions that might suggest to the dramatist another source for the technique of multiple mansion staging. Up to this point action has been centered in the church, and the Ordo specifically calls for recitation of the psalter "in choro." Yet in the margin of Codex Casinensis 198, the notation after Terce is "let them go to the cemetery reciting psalms for the dead in a low voice and then to the chapter house." Leuterman observes, "to judge from the characteristics of the writing, this insertion is from the thirteenth century."[37] He offers no opinion whether the insertion represents a new development in the ceremonies that was contemporary with the notation or a correction which records long-standing practice.

36. Ibid., p. 53.
37. Ibid., p. 54.

Whatever its date, the insertion makes it apparent that the community's devotion expands time and space. The procession to the cemetery extends the boundaries of the allegorical Mount Sinai and distinguishes it from profane space. The singing enlarges the community and removes it from secular history, so that it joins an eternal community of worshippers. In the observances designated for the chapter house, ceremonies amplify the role of this community as witness and participant. In the course of the observances, the community acts out the burial and resurrection. "Terce being finished, let them go to the chapter house and let there be a reading from the martyrology: *Saturday, Our Lord remained in the sepulchre.* Let all of them throw themselves on the ground and thus let each one say to himself the verse for breaking silence. Then, when the abbot rises, let them rise and be seated. The lector shall read the lessons according to custom. The lessons being finished, let the abbot say, *Adiutorium nostrum.* And immediately rising, let them go out in silence and throughout the whole day let no one speak in the cloister and let them remain barefoot." In its movement as well as its utterances the community is continually drawn into a broader participation in the observances. The meditative character of the services gives way to enactment, as the area of ritual expands from church to cemetery to chapter house and finally to the cloisters.

At the end of Sext the literal and figurative evocations of the Passion converge in the reading of Mark's Passion narrative, and the different episodes of the Passion sequence which had been connected to each other in a musical structure now emerge in a complete framework. If the gospel reading establishes the full dimensions of the Passion as narrative, the ceremony immediately following fixes its mimetic qualities. "This finished, all the crosses are uncovered, and the

crosses from the Lord's Cross are prepared before the altar
with enough space from the altar so that meanwhile anyone
who wishes may adore them freely and privately up to the
hour of the offices." The crosses here are central objects of
meditation, and later ceremonies will exploit the emotional
power of the cross as relic and commemorative object when
the feast moves even further from private devotion to public
adoration. Between the unveiling of the crosses and the beginning of these public commemorative ceremonies, the hour
of Nones intervenes. The antiphon defines its major action by
recalling the climactic moment of the sacrifice: "Jesus crying
in a loud voice sent forth his spirit, and the veil of the temple
has been torn." Meanwhile the psalm verse "Wonderful are
your decrees; therefore I observe them" (Psalm 118:129)
identifies the community as the other focal point of liturgical
action.

The Good Friday ritual which begins after the ninth hour
marks the expansion of representational features of liturgy
and proves thereby more immediately useful to a dramatist's
sense of action and spectacle. In the first part of the office,
figural and literal evocations of the Passion continue; however, with the reading from John the office approaches the
representational modes which Hardison defines as the drama
of the early Middle Ages. The preparatory phase of the ceremonies is designed in its details to commemorate the death of
Christ. The celebrant and his ministers enter a space which is
consciously austere. "Let the celebrant go from the sacristy
with his ministers dressed in black chasibules and barefoot.
And coming before the altar, prostrating themselves on the
ground, let them pray for a long time. Then arising and kissing the altar, let them go to be seated, and let a small cloth

be placed on the altar under the Gospel book, and let a candle be lit before the altar until the end of the office." After the preparation of the altar the subdeacon reads a passage from Hosea (6:1–6) which prefigures the redemption and a tract whose accompanying verses point to the Crucifixion in phrases such as "between two animals," taken to represent the two thieves at the Crucifixion. The second reading, by another subdeacon, recalls the institution of the paschal feast among the Hebrews (Exodus 12:1–11).

After the second tract the subdeacon begins John's Passion gospel in an setting specifically directed by the Ordo: "Let no incense or light be carried in front of the Gospel." His singing, Willi Apel observes, is "designed to bring out contrast between the participants of the story: Christ, the Jews, and the Evangelist who narrates the events. This was done by providing for a recitation at three different pitch levels and speeds, low and slow for the words of Christ, high and fast for those of the Jews, and medium for those of the Evangelist."[38] The singing is accompanied by action which demonstrates the possibilities of enactment in the office and establishes the worship on a middle ground between devotion and drama. "When the deacon shall come to the place in the Passion where it is said, 'My vestments are divided,' these subdeacons who are vested with the celebrant shall immediately strip the altar, in the manner of thieves, of the cloth which had earlier been placed under the Gospel." Hardison and Leuterman relate the stripping of the altar to observances recorded in Gregory the Great's first Roman Ordo, but they differ in interpretation. Hardison cites the tradition of Amal-

38. Willi Apel, *Gregorian Chant* (Bloomington: Indiana University Press, 1958), p. 209.

arius where the action is "a commemoration of the flight of the apostles."[39] For Leuterman, "the altar with the Gospel book represents Christ from whom the clothes are taken 'in the manner of thieves.' "[40] In either tradition, the gesture recurs to the symbolic world which underlies what Hardison terms "rememorative allegory."

The Adoratio crucis also combines singing and liturgical action, but it directs them equally toward the Passion and the present reality of worship. The ceremony was developed within the Jerusalem Church. The *Peregrinatio Egeriae* records a ceremony which in its essential actions closely resembles the observances held on Good Friday at Montecassino. Leuterman argues the adoration was known in Rome as early as the fifth century; Karl Young dates its introduction in the West during the seventh or eighth century. Gregory's first Roman Ordo describes an adoration ceremony in connection with the feast, as does a ninth-century Ordo from Einsiedeln which seems to be the basis of the Cassinese rite.[41] The adoration begins after the reading of John's gospel and the prayers for the church. The priest taking the cross held by the two acolytes intones the antiphon, "Behold the wood of the Cross on which the salvation of the world hung." When he says, "Come, let us adore," the faithful kneel and adore the cross; rising they repeat the antiphon and begin to recite Psalm 118 ("Beati immaculati"), alternating the antiphon with each verse of the psalm. During this recital, the priest makes his own adoration, after which the community in order

39. Hardison, *Christian Rite and Christian Drama in the Middle Ages*, p. 130.

40. *Ordo*, p. 61.

41. Ibid., p. 64; Karl Young, *The Drama of the Medieval Church* (Oxford: Clarendon Press, 1933), I, 102.

of seniority begins to make its adoration. In groups of five or six, the faithful prostrate themselves and each recites to himself at the first prostration "Domine Iesu Christe Deus verus de Deo vero," the prayer which emphasizes Christ's triumph over the ignominy of the Cross and his power to gird the suppliant for battle against enemies. At the second prostration, the group recites the prayer "Deus qui Moysi famulo tuo" and at the third "Domine Iesu Christe qui nos per passionem crucem," which again looks forward to mankind's liberation through the Cross. After the genuflections, the monks kneel before the cross, touch their heads to the ground, and sing "We adore your Cross, Lord, and we glorify your holy resurrection; come, people, let us adore the resurrection of Christ." They then kiss the cross, genuflect, and retire as the next group approaches.

After six or eight verses of Psalm 118 have been repeated in alternation with the antiphon "Ecce lignum crucis," three clerics vested in albs approach the cross and begin the Trisagion. The clerics sing the Greek verses, and the chorus replies to each one of them with the Latin equivalent:

Clerici: Agyos o Theos.   *Clerici*: Agyos athanatos.
Chorus: Sanctus Deus.   *Chorus*: Sanctus immortalis.
Clerici: Agyos ischiros.   *Clerici*: Eleyson ymas.
Chorus: Sanctus fortis.   *Chorus*: Miserere nobis.

These same three clerics then begin the *improperia* which commemorate Christ's reproaches from the Cross. The Ordo stresses their commemorative function by placing the recitation in front of the cross.

Verse: My people, what did I do to you? Or how did I bring you sorrow? Will you tell me? Because I led you out of the land of Egypt, you made ready a cross for your Savior.

Verse: Because I led you through the desert for forty years and gave you manna to eat and led you into the best land, you made ready a cross for your Savior.

Verse: What else should I have done for you and did not do? I planted for you my most precious vine, and you have become overly bitter to me. For you sated your thirst with vinegar, and pierced the side of your Savior with a lance.

In the rite formulated by Gregory the Great and in the Gallican usage of Amalarius, the *improperia* end with this last verse. However, the twelfth-century Cassinese Ordo requires a continuation of the *improperia*. Three other clerics in similar dress approach the cross and begin with the verse "Ego propter te flagellavi." In alternation with each verse the chorus repeats the first antiphon, "Popule meus quid feci tibi?" This divergence from Roman usage underscores an interest in the ceremony that might be one source of inspiration for a dramatist. The verses which continue the *improperia* offer an extended description of the Crucifixion as well as typological connections between the scene and the Old Testament.

On account of you I scourged Egypt with its first born, and you betrayed me when I was scourged.

I led you forth from Egypt, having drowned Pharaoh in the Red Sea, and you betrayed me to the leaders of the priests.

I opened the sea before you, and you opened my side with a lance.

I went before you in a column of clouds, and you led me to the courtyard to Pilate.

I sent you manna in the desert, and you fell on me with fists and whips.

I provided you with the water of salvation from the rock, and you gave me gall and vinegar to drink.

For you I struck down the kings of the Chanaanites, and you beat my head with reeds.

I gave you the royal scepter, and you gave a crown of thorns for my head.

I raised you in great virtue, and you hanged me from a cross.

At the end of the *improperia* yet another group of three clerics, again dressed in albs, comes before the cross and begins the antiphon "Crux fidelis":

True cross, among every kind the noble tree: no tree puts forth so much in leaf, flower, and seed. Sweet wood, sweet nails hold up the sweet weight.

The chorus replies "Crux fidelis," and the three clerics begin to sing the "Pange lingua" with the chorus repeating "Crux fidelis" at the end of each verse. At the conclusion the celebrant and his ministers put on their shoes, wash their hands, and retire to the sacristy to prepare for the Mass of the Presanctified.

If the combination of music with liturgical action suggests a movement in the Good Friday ceremonies that tends toward representation, the music for the Adoratio crucis points as well toward an historical continuity between the monastic community and earlier worshippers. The Trisagion was in use by the Council of Chalcedon (451), and the Council of Vaison (529) permitted it to be sung in all Masses. The *improperia* derive from twelve Troparia attributed to Sophronios, patriarch of Jerusalem (634–38), which are among the oldest pieces of Byzantine hymnography. The "Crucem tuam adoramus, Domine" is a translation of an earlier Byzantine composition, and the Latin version follows the same basic melody. Two eleventh-century Beneventan troparia (Benevento, Biblioteca Capitolare, VI. 38 and VI. 40) contain even more bilingual songs, but the music indicated by the twelfth-century Cassinese Ordo itself reflects the return to origins. Wellesz points out, "from these hymns a line can be drawn forward to the present-day restricted use of Greek words during the *Adoratio Crucis*, and also backward to the liturgical ceremony on Good Friday at Jerusalem in the age of the *Peregrinatio Aetheriae*; that is, to the end of the fourth century, which marks the beginning of the development of all ecclesiastical institutions."[42] Thus as the offices move toward the structure of drama, they also imply a broader concept of imitation which joins communities of worshippers in a sense of liturgy.

In the Adoration rite, the cross establishes similar connections between liturgical action and dramatic representation. As a stage property, it is the focus of representational action. Hardison says, "the cross ceases to be a simple object of meditation. It is treated as the original Cross, and two deacons, standing in the darkness behind it, supply reproaches (*improperia*) understood to be spoken by Christ himself. Meanwhile priest and chorus reply in the manner of a tragic chorus."[43] The antitheses of the *improperia* lead from redemption to alienation, as the responsorial form repeats the question, "Quid feci tibi?" But set against this alienation are the assertions of praise and celebration in the Trisagion. Whereas the *improperia* give prominence to Christ's abasement, helplessness, and mortality, the verses of the Trisagion unite Latin and the earlier universal language of the church to affirm holiness, strength, and immortality. In this process, as Leuterman observes, "Christ is newly refigured as a victim for the sinners: for them he is constrained to suffer and

42. Wellesz, *Eastern Elements in Western Chant*, p. 18.
43. Hardison, *Christian Rite and Christian Drama in the Middle Ages*, p. 131.

to bear humiliation; but there is always the response, 'Holy God, Holy Strength, Holy Immortality. Have mercy on us.' "[44] The abasement of the Crucifixion becomes in the *Pange lingua* a "noble triumph" and the cross becomes the "sweet wood." Still, the dialectic of alienation and redemption is not resolved here so much as exaggerated to the point where resolution becomes necessary. Such resolution will be achieved in the liturgical pattern that continues on after the celebration of the Good Friday offices and the performance of the Passion drama.

A long history connects the drama to liturgy. The reappearance of drama in the West during the tenth century is commonly attributed to changes in practice in the liturgical offices. In the same period, commentators on ritual start to explain the Mass in terms that emphasize its dramatic qualities. For later writers, liturgy remains a source for thematic inspiration, but its relation to drama undergoes a substantial modification. The drama of the twelfth century relies on ritual not as a source but as a context for defining its own conventions. The Limoges *Sponsus* and the Anglo-Norman *Jeu d'Adam* are often described as "semi-liturgical," though historians are unsure what feasts were connected with the plays.[45] The first Passion play was written in an era immediately following efforts to centralize liturgy and reform earlier practices. One important link between this reformed liturgy and the play is the element of music. Music offers a structure that complements the doctrinal features of both ritual and drama. Medieval musical theory asserts the power of song

44. *Ordo*, p. 66.
45. See, for example, Gustave Cohen, *Anthologie du drame liturgique en France au Moyen-Age* (Paris: Éditions du Cerf, 1955), pp. 259–60.

to image cosmic order. In liturgy, this power joins with the belief in prayer and spiritual sacrifice. In drama, it supports the attempt to devise a structure for expressing the transcendent as well as the historical aspects of the Biblical narrative. For all these resemblances, however, the differences between drama and liturgy remain essential. From the outset, the drama connects itself to the commemorative observances of the divine offices and not to the Mass itself. The reason for doing so lies in the drama's supplementing the Mass rather than replacing it.

5. The Passion Play and the Poetics of Medieval Drama

T HE COMPOSITION of a Passion play in the twelfth century forces us to modify many of the approaches we take toward the medieval drama. Above all, the ideology of the Passion play shows the need for a critical method that recognizes the dual nature of the church-drama. The preceding chapters have emphasized the drama's incorporation of iconography and music as a strategy for presenting the transcendent aspect of its topic. To the extent that medieval views of art and music derive from a Neoplatonic rationale, the critic is led to suspend the assumptions of Aristotelian criticism and to examine the drama in a more suitable framework. Still, the claims of transcendence are only one aspect of the early medieval drama. The achievement of the Montecassino author and other writers lies in joining the transcendent to the historical. The use of legal conventions and the recasting of Scripture into contemporary verse give the first Passion drama an historical, recurrent feature. The alternation of Latin and the vernacular indicates the historical element in other works. This element can be approached through a modified Aristotelian system, though the approach is necessarily limited in several respects. It must take into account the considerable redefinition an element like spectacle undergoes during the

Middle Ages. Moreover, it proves most useful in areas where the drama either deals with recurrence or treats unique events as if they were recurrent. In the Passion play, these areas involve techniques of staging, especially as they affect character, thought, and diction. In restructuring the traditional categories, the Montecassino text offers a distinct perspective on the poetics of medieval drama.

In the *Poetics* (VI) Aristotle lists spectacle among the external parts of tragedy and remarks that it "has, indeed, an emotional attraction of its own, but, of all the parts, it is the least artistic, and connected least with the art of poetry."[1] Accordingly, he consigns a work like *Prometheus Bound* to the fourth and lowest category of tragedy, the tragedy of spectacle. O. B. Hardison, Jr., notes in his commentary on the *Poetics* that "The interest of such a play is its appeal, written or performed, to the visual imagination."[2] Early Christian writers treat the effects of this appeal from a different viewpoint, and they tend to reverse Aristotle's hierarchy of elements. For them, spectacle is an aspect of witnessing. St. Paul views martyrdom as a spectacle for angels and men. He says, "For I think God has set forth us the apostles last of all, as men doomed to death, seeing that we have been made a spectacle to the world, and to angels, and to men" (1 Corinthians 4:9). In the second century, Tertullian's *De spectaculis* makes a major attack on the pagan theater, circus, and games. In place of the pagan excesses, Tertullian proposes a Christian literature where the spectacular effects occur within the mind of the reader. "If the literature of the stage delight you, we have sufficiency of books, of poems, of aphorisms,

1. *Aristotle's Poetics*, trans. H. H. Butcher, intro. Francis Fergusson (New York: Hill and Wang, 1961), p. 64.
2. *Aristotle's Poetics*, eds. Leon Golden and O. B. Hardison, Jr. (Englewood Cliffs: Prentice Hall, 1968), p. 236.

sufficiency of songs and voices, not fable, those of ours, but truth; not artifice but simplicity."[3]

As Rosemary Woolf points out, two traditions follow from these writers. "One kept close to Paul in finding the comparison in the virtuous life: according to St Bernard, for instance, the *bonus ludus* is that which provides a pleasing spectacle to the heavenly audience; most undeserving of the title of *ludus* are the contortions of the contemporary entertainers, the *ioculatores* and *saltatores*. The other followed Tertullian in finding the source of the spectacle in the torments of the damned."[4] A miniature in the Cassinese transcription (c. 1023) of Rabanus Maurus's *De universo* shows the vitality of the second tradition. The miniature depicts male figures in a grandstand applauding an actor who sheathes his sword while behind him two decapitated men fall forward. The illustration accompanies Rabanus' definition of *theatrum* and carries out its mystical sense. "The theater is given its name from spectacle *apo tes theorias*, because in it the people, standing above and looking, watch the plays. This same theater is indeed a brothel, because after the plays let out prostitutes go on sale. And it is called a brothel on account of these very prostitutes, who because of the vileness of their notorious flesh are called by the name wolves. For the wolves are called prostitutes on account of their greed because they will drag the wretched to them and seize them. In fact, the brothels were built by pagans, so that the shame of barren women might be made known there, and they who built it might be held in mockery as much as those who are exposed. In a mystical sense, however, the theater can mean the present

3. Tertullian, *De spectaculis*, trans. T. R. Glover, Loeb Classical Library (Cambridge, Mass.: Harvard University Press, 1931), pp. 296–97.
4. Rosemary Woolf, *The English Mystery Plays* (Berkeley and Los Angeles: University of California Press, 1972), p. 31.

world, in which those who follow the luxury of this world hold the servants of God in shame, and delight in watching their sufferings."[5] The staging techniques of the church-drama seem to bear out the emphases of Christian spectacle. Paul, Tertullian, and Rabanus insist on the public character of suffering and on the role of judgment. One must witness the action directly and recognize its moral implications. For the dramatists who follow in the tradition, the redefinition of spectacle requires a special attention to the details of performance. The rubrics of early liturgical drama set down guidelines for performance with the same precision that the liturgical Ordo employs to prescribe the action of ritual. The Montecassino Passion shows this precision in both its stage directions and expositions. Paolo Toschi observes that the play "exhibits a scenic appeal of notable complexity and variety."[6] Sandro Sticca notes that "the wealth of rubrics, prescribing movement, gesture, and facial expression, point out our dramatist's concern for the performance of his play."[7] Omer Jodogne draws attention to the artistry of the mute scene where a devil appears to Pilate's wife as Christ is beaten.[8]

The concern with spectacle also allows some modification to the circumstances of production. In the Montecassino play, these circumstances influence part of the staging technique. The primary audience is a monastic community, and the ex-

5. Rabanus Maurus, *De universo*, xx. 36, in *Patrologia Latina*, ed. J.-P. Migne (Paris, 1852), CXI, 553.
6. Paolo Toschi, "Bibliografia," *Archivum Romanicum* 21 (1937), 399.
7. Sandro Sticca, *The Latin Passion Play: Its Origins and Development* (Albany: State University of New York Press, 1970), p. 105.
8. Omer Jodogne, "Le plus ancien Mystère de la Passion," *Académie Royale des sciences, des lettres et des beaux arts de Belgique. Classe des lettres et des sciences morales et politiques. Bulletin.* 5e serie., 50 (1964), 3–14.

positions adapt to the audience as much as to the general considerations of uniqueness and recurrence. The audience is already initiated into the mysteries that the play seeks to dramatize, and it is aware of such elements as plot and character. Hence, the staging techniques are closer to recall than to normal exposition. Rather than create scenes and characters solely within the play, the dramatist allows his audience to identify them from its own experience. These exchanges and responses between the work and its audience imply a process of recurrence and direct one to an element of stylization, which is perhaps most evident in the play's processions where Christ is led bound from one mansion to another. But in addition to the fully initiated, the play will presumably instruct the novice; as such, it must present the unique and transcendent events to him as if they were recurrent. For this reason, the playwright is careful to soften the uniqueness by amplifying the conventional nature of the drama's action. The inclusion of a vernacular *planctus* indicates a degree of lay participation, and this development further obliges the author to define and explain the action he selects. To satisfy these diverse requirements, the playwright exerts a considerable flexibility in presenting the stage action. For his expositions, he has the option of using a narrator-stage director to explain dramatic action in the way later vernacular works present an expositor. He can also integrate exposition and stage action so that the movements in the play are connected to a verbal definition. The text shows that he decides for the second of these alternatives and allows the play's characters to define both their own actions and those of others.

A system of autocommentary or "glossing" as a way to deal with what might be the work's uniqueness develops in the process of dramatic action as the personae label what they do. The concept of glossing, as Georg Goetz indicates, may be traced to Quintillian's *Institutio oratoria* (I. 1, 35) where *glossa* means the elucidation of obscure terms.[9] Quintillian's work regained its stature in the twelfth century, above all in the school of Chartres, and Alan de Lille uses the verb *glossare* in his *Anticlaudianus* and *De planctu naturae* to mean 'uncovering' and 'opening, as a gloss reveals the force of the word.'[10] John V. Fleming finds an expanded sense of the term in such narrative works. "The technical term 'gloss,' of course, by no means always refers to the allegorical unveiling of cryptic meaning. One of its common medieval meanings is simply *explication de texte*, amplification or paraphrase on the literal level."[11] The Montecassino playwright, drawing on narrative sources in the Vulgate, uses this expanded sense of the term as one aspect of his dramaturgy. For example, as Peter strikes off Malchus' ear in the play, he tells him, "now I'll make you deaf" (vv. 56–57). The witnesses who offer false testimony in the scene between Christ and Caiaphas similarly paraphrase their actions and roles. Before they give testimony, they identify themselves, "hear us, you people standing around here, for we are giving true testimony" (vv. 76–78).

The reciprocal nature of the identification proves an interesting feature of the dramatist's technique, for it brings

9. Georg Goetz, *De glossariorum latinorum origine et fatis* (Leipzig: B. G. Teubner, 1923). Leo Spitzer discusses these sources and their influence in the Middle Ages in "The Prologue to the *Lais* of Marie de France and Medieval Poetics," *Modern Philology* 41 (1943–44), 96–102; rpt. in *Romanische Literaturstudien: 1936–1956* (Tübingen: Max Niemeyer Verlag, 1959), pp. 3–14.

10. C. Du Cange, *Glossarium ad Scriptores mediae et infimae Latinitatis* (1678; rpt. Niort: L. Favre, 1883–87), s.v. *glossare*.

11. John V. Fleming, *The Roman de la Rose: A Study on Allegory and Iconography* (Princeton: Princeton University Press, 1969), p. 7.

out the moral dimensions of spectacle. The line of exposition moves to include the audience as well as to further the narrative. As the witnesses identify themselves, they also describe the roles of the other personae on stage and of their audience. The other personae and the audience bear witness to the action, and the fidelity of the play's representation constitutes a "true testimony." At such moments, the drama approaches the conditions of metatheater. The expositions not only define the literal content of the scene but also assert the credibility of the work as a faithful reproduction of the Passion. The choral voice ("we are giving true testimony" [*sumus confirmantes*]) is not that of the two witnesses alone; it is, in addition, the collective statement of the players and the audience in their multiple roles as witnesses against Christ and as participants in the testimony and the play. The autocommentary of dramatic exposition connects the unique event to a form based on recurrence and so draws attention to both the scene and the act of perceiving it. By so doing, the separation of art and life space which the proscenium stage defines is eliminated and the rigid formalism of Aristotelian dramatic categories is attenuated.

In depicting Christ's physical ordeal, the Montecassino Passion like later vernacular works is careful to exhibit the full details of suffering. It does so by emphasizing the resemblances between the speeches and the stage directions as modes of discourse. The speeches of the torturers restate the actions prescribed in the rubrics. After Caiaphas rips his own garments in outrage at Christ's assertion of divinity, the soldiers beat Christ and spit in his face. The text reads:

Then let the armed men answer against Jesus in a loud voice and let them strike him and spit in his face and say:

165

Let the defendant be put to death. Let his neck bow under the blows.

(vv. 97–98)

As the soldiers conduct Christ to Pilate's court, they take over as stage directors, again describing their own action ("let the armed men lead Jesus bound before Pilate") with the lines, "Let us lead Jesus tightly bound to Pilate, ruler of the Jews" (vv. 139–41). Then, amplifying their role, they describe the flagellation scene which will take place only after Pilate's interrogation: "Let us bind Jesus to the pillar, sinking to his ruin, a hostage to death" (vv. 142–44). The language of these lines is closely allied to the grammar of the rubrics. The stage directions appear in the subjunctive mood to describe the visual composition of the play as well as to relate the episode to the dramatist's intention. Implicit in this intention is a function of anticipation. The rubrics set out the ideal shape of action, and the dialogue and speeches of the play give it an historical enactment.

The York *Crucifixion* pageant, whose realism modern critics have stressed, provides a helpful contrast for understanding the element of spectacle in the Montecassino Passion.[12] The York play has a different grammar for its stagecraft. For the subjunctive and future tenses of the Montecassino text, it uses another descriptive system. The effect of this shift is a precise demonstration of the mechanics of Crucifixion, as the soldiers say to one another:

> *ii Mil.* Nowe, certis, I schall noȝt feyne
> Or his right hande be feste.

12. For recent views, see J. W. Robinson, "The Art of the York Realist," *Modern Philology* 60 (1962–63), 241–51; Clifford Davidson, "The Realism of the York Realist and the York Passion," *Speculum* 50 (1975), 270–83.

iii Mil. þe left hande þanne is myne,
Late see who beres hym beste.
iv Mil. Hys lymmys on lenght þan schalle I lede,
And even vnto þe bore þame bringe,
i. Mil. Vnto his heede I schall take hede,
And with myne helpe hymn to hyng.[13]

The Montecassino playwright is no less exact in defining every act suffered by Christ in the pretorium, but his stress is on the implication of spectacle and staging. The distinctions of the play's grammar allow him to present intention and action as the scene moves from a stylized mocking to a catalogue of abuse and destruction.

Let this Jesus be stripped of his clothing and let him put on a scarlet robe. Let us honor him on our knees and let us wreath him with a crown of thorns. Let us mock him greatly, spit in his face, putting a reed in his right hand.

(vv. 274–82)

The scenes of the buffeting and crucifixion demonstrate again the reciprocal nature of language in the Passion play. The dramatist is conscious of both the stage action and the audience. The stage directions for the buffeting call for the soldiers to place the reed in Christ's hand and to spit in his face: "Here let them put the reed in Jesus' hand and spit in his face." However, the full visual image appears only when the soldiers explain their intentions and actions to the audience: "Let us punish Jesus harshly. Let us beat and strike his brow back and front" (vv. 283–85). In the preparations for the crucifixion, the soldiers also narrate toward dual ends. Although the passage is defective in the manuscript, in the surviving text they anticipate the play's subsequent action

13. Pageant XXXV, vv. 80–88, in *York Plays*, ed. Lucy Toulmin Smith (1885; rpt. New York: Russell and Russell, 1963).

before Christ begins the *via crucis*: "let us crucify Jesus on Mount Calvary" (vv. 290–91).

In glossing the text and relating intention to action, the play's language combines categories of works that an art historian like André Grabar finds distinct even in paleochristian art. "A distinction is generally not made between works that serve practical ends—those which, in the realm of imagery, fix and transmit facts or ideas—and images that interpret these facts and these ideas in poetic fashion through procedures that are essentially aesthetic. We are wrong in thus confounding informative images and expressive images. The first appeal solely to the intellect (exactly like a technical text), while the others make an appeal to the imagination and the aesthetic sense."[14] The play's joining of informative and expressive images balances the empathetic movement of the action with a movement toward transcendence. As the scenes unfold, the playwright refers action back not only to previous scenes but to models in iconography. The glossing consequently emphasizes the ties between the play and ecclesiastical art, where such labelling is a common technique of exposition and instruction.

These countermovements achieve a special stylization in passages where the dramatic figures preface the glosses with versions of the phrase *ecce facio*. Here the speakers define dramatic action as they signal to an audience the process of exposition. When Caiaphas tears his garment in rage and says, "ecce scindo tunicam" ("Look, I tear the tunic"—v. 96), he places his own action in heightened relief and conveys simultaneously the gesture and the appropriate label. The soldiers'

14. André Grabar, *Christian Iconography: A Study of Its Origins*, trans. Terry Grabar, Bollingen Series, XXXV, A. W. Mellon Lectures in the Fine Arts, X (Princeton: Princeton University Press, 1968), p. xliv.

exposition as they lead Christ to Caiaphas relates the counter-movements of narrative and glossing to dramatic anticipation. Such anticipation separates the ongoing movement of the drama into discrete gestures. The soldiers state their planned action and sketch the scene that will follow from it.

> Ecce Iesum teneamus
> quem ligatum perducamus
> Cayphe in atrium.
> Ubi populi maiores
> scribe nec non seniores
> faciunt concilium.
>   (vv. 70–5)

Look, we have Jesus whom we lead bound into the courtyard of Caiaphas where the leaders of the people, the scribes, and elders hold council.

They repeat the formula in presenting Christ to Pilate (vv. 151–3), and Pilate hands Christ over to the priests, saying, "ecce Iesum flagellatum / vobis trado condempnatum" ("Look at Jesus scourged. I give him to you condemned"— vv. 268–9).

In conveying this sequence of images, the playwright breaks the naturalistic illusion which the recurrent character of drama imposes on action and movement. Much as the characters' expositions permit anticipation by dissolving one image into the next, the fragmenting of action allows the focus to return to an earlier scene. The stylization and the grammatical distinctions of Peter's lament show this reversal and point up again the dual nature of church-drama.

Three times I denied Jesus and now the cock has crowed. Look, I cry bitterly now. My tongue denied him whom I had promised to love.

The Latin text reads:

> Iesum tertio negavi
>   et nunc gallus cecinit.
> Ecce fleo nunc amare
> quem promiseram amare,
>   mea lingua renuit.
>   (vv. 122–26)

The lament joins the iconic image of Peter weeping to the earlier image of his denial of Christ by shading the meanings of the preterite. The aorist sense of "Three times I denied" (*tertio negavi*) leads to the true perfect of "now the cock has crowed" (*nunc gallus cecinit*). So the unique action of Peter is opposed to a pattern of recurrence in the natural world. The adverb *nunc* links the preterite form to the glossed image "Look, I cry bitterly now" (*Ecce fleo nunc amare*), and the interplay of *amarē*, 'bitterly,' and *amāre*, 'to love,' connects the image of weeping to the earlier promise to love Christ. The lament is a set piece whose circular patterns suggests miniature art: it opens with the aorist preterite, then moves to the true preterite, present, and past perfect tenses, and closes with the aorist preterite. Although the grammatical distinctions may locate action on a natural and causal level, they dissolve with the repetition of *nunc* and *amare*, and the playwright reconstructs the image of Peter weeping along the lines of his own rhetorical model.

The fragmentation allows the dramatist to set out a more ambitious program of staging than traditional Aristotelian conventions might otherwise permit. The rubrics prescribe a number of *mansions* or *sedes*. Action often occurs simultaneously among them, and in several instances mute scenes serve as backgrounds for the main dramatic action. Sticca observes that the play uses a total of eight separate *sedes*: "the

Garden of Gethsemane, referred to as 'locum ubi orat Iesus', Caiaphas' house, a place for the disciples to hide, Pilate's house, the column where Jesus is flagellated. Also there must be: appropriate *sedes* where Pilate's wife is to sleep, a Pretorium called *alium locum*, the Calvary referred to as 'locum ubi [Iesus] debet crucifigi'."[15] Although this program is elaborate in the way that later continental drama will duplicate, the sense of stage remains controlled and focused, and reveals as much in its exclusion of material as in selection. Whereas a work such as the Chester *Passion* includes an interview with Herod, the Montecassino play maintains dramatic tension through confrontations with only two judges, Caiaphas and Pilate. The Sulmona fragment, which shares some sixty lines with the Cassinese text, shows the soldiers hurled to the ground in the betrayal scene, but the Montecassino playwright avoids such extravagant material and portrays the apocryphal apparition of the devil to Procula without dialogue.

The exclusion of the marvelous permits the dramatist to explore the connection between character and setting. Caiaphas asserts his role as a spiritual judge and the suppression of an interview with Herod suggests that the courts of Caiaphas and Pilate are mirror images of each other. Staging also allows the dramatist to embellish his characterization of Peter. After Peter finishes his lamentation, he joins the other disciples who have abandoned Christ and fled from his presence. In some measure, the flexibility of multiple mansion staging might seem to raise a problem of dramatic unity. Much as glossing disperses the movement of narrative, the division into iconic scenes on different *sedes* would seem to

15. Sandro Sticca, "The Priority of the Montecassino Passion Play," *Latomus* 20 (1961), 834.

reduce plot to a series of disparate visual images. Glynne Wickham discusses the same problem in connection with late medieval pageantry and royal entries, where separate acting areas in a city correspond to the multiple mansions of drama. Wickham finds that actors and authors "derived a corresponding advantage from this unusual disposition of scenes on independent and isolated stages: for, what was said both verbally and visually in each tableau was addressed directly at the person thus honoured and his retinue. His or her presence before each of the tableaux in turn provided a common link between them all. The effect was inevitably to endow the pageants with a unity of theme instead of the unity usually discernible in plot or through character."[16] The nature of these representations is to portray dramatic scenes and to present an oratorical address.

The thematic unity is evident in the Montecassino Passion, although the oratory remains within the play and does not become self-reflexive. The figure of Christ, like the personage honored in pageantry, connects the events acted out on different *sedes*. In the extant text, Christ is never absent from the stage, and even in such scenes as Judas' bargain and Procula's dream where he has no speaking part, the actions and choices of the other characters constitute a response to his assertion of divinity. The recurrence of this dramatic situation in different locales fuses the scenes which the dramatist selects from his narrative sources, although in Aristotelian terms the result may still be "episodic."

Simultaneous staging develops easily from the use of multiple mansions. Grace Frank argues that the device is pervasive in medieval drama. It offers the playwright a second series

16. Glynne Wickham, *Early English Stages 1300–1660* (London: Routledge and Kegan Paul, 1959), I, 59.

of technical advantages. "It made possible a splendid and highly diversified spectacle. It allowed the action of the play to move from station to station without scene-shifting so that the sequence of events could proceed without breaking the illusion no matter where the action occurred. At need action could even go forward in different places simultaneously. Above all, in the religious plays, such staging kept a synthesis of the play's meaning constantly before the audience."[17] Gustave Cohen finds two principles extant in the earliest medieval dramatic texts: "The first of these principles requires that all the different places where action occurs successively be juxtaposed; the second of these principles requires that the spectator move along the length of these fixed settings as the action advances from one point to another of the world then known and compactly depicted on a scaffold some meters long."[18] The Montecassino Passion makes use of the simultaneous action arising from such staging to contrast and parallel individual scenes. In so doing, it establishes a system of contiguity to augment the systems of sequence and temporality which dominate classical drama.

The device first appears in the events preceding the arrest in Gethsemane where it enforces the Christian redefinition of spectacle. After Judas strikes his bargain with Caiaphas and receives soldiers to accomplish the seizure, he arranges a signal with them to identify Christ. The stage directions indicate that his actions take place as Christ continues to pray on Mount Olivet: "Then let Judas go out with the armed

17. Grace Frank, *The Medieval French Drama* (Oxford: Clarendon Press, 1954), pp. 90–91.
18. Gustave Cohen, *Histoire de la mise en scène dans le théâtre religieux Français du Moyen Age*, rev. ed. (Paris: Librairie Champion, 1951), p. 70. A more recent discussion of staging and acting areas appears in Fletcher Collins, *The Production of Medieval Church-Drama* (Charlottesville, Virginia: University Press of Virginia, 1972), pp. 24–34.

men and, holding council with them, let him go to the place where Jesus is praying." Because the text preceding the bargain scene is missing, it is difficult to speculate on what constitutes the beginning of the play. However, an agony scene is quite probable; and it continues, perhaps in pantomime, through Judas' meeting with Caiaphas, to contrast Christ's assertion of faith with Judas' denial of belief in him. The flight of the apostles at the seizure amplifies the dramatic possibilities of the staging technique. Their flight and later reunion with Peter establish a space where the play turns in on itself. Like the false witnesses at the trial, they are witnesses who stand also as surrogates for the audience. Thus the audience responds to images of both the Passion and itself in the act of viewing the Passion play.

The staging further delineates the character of Peter by suggesting parallels with Christ and Judas. In the mocking scene the primary ordeal suffered by Christ is verbal rather than physical; after the soldiers buffet Christ, they challenge him, saying, "Prophesy to us, now, Christ; tell us who just hit you" (vv. 100–102). Peter undergoes a similar ordeal with the maid who questions him about Christ. The play's rubrics link these two episodes: "While these things written above are being done and while the false witnesses are accusing Jesus before Caiaphas, let the maid cry against Peter." Peter's lament after this scene sets in motion one of the most technically complex scenes in early medieval drama. As he joins the disciples in hiding, Christ is led from Caiaphas' house to Pilate's *sedes*: "During this time let Jesus be taken from the presence of Caiaphas and let them lead him bound before Pilate." While these actions are carried out, Judas confronts the high priests and attempts to return the coins: "Also while Peter is lamenting, let Judas carry back the coins and

174

throw them on a table in front of Caiaphas." The play later
confirms the simultaneity of these scenes by directing after
the return of the coins: "and Judas goes out and hangs himself. Meanwhile let the armed men lead Jesus bound before
Pilate." Judas' exit confirms the importance of dramatic space
in the play, for by moving out of the major playing areas he
leaves Jerusalem, which in typology and the literature of
pilgrimage is the *axis mundi*. The possibilities of staging thus
allow the playwright to remove his characters from a central
area and to offer a symmetrical composition. Christ becomes
the focal point, and flanking him are characters who view
themselves as traitors and admit individually, "Oh, how
deeply I have sinned" (vv. 121, 128).

The scene with Pilate's wife calls for an equal skill in man-
aging stage areas. The rubrics direct that Christ stand bound
to a column during the entire scene:

Let Jesus answer nothing to this but be taken from the presence of
Pilate while his wife sleeps, and he is tied to a pillar and let him be
whipped. and let Jesus stand bound until the maid returns from Pilate.
While the things written above are being done all the while that
Jesus stands bound to the pillar let Pilate's wife sleep. and let a devil
appear to her as she sleeps in her dreams.

A sense of discontinuity pervades the scene and highlights the
element of spectacle. First of all, Christ is flagellated as Procula tells the maid to warn her husband, "Let him not bother
that just man, sublime in his miracles, a magnificent prophet"
(vv. 175–77). So the stage action contradicts Procula's warning in precisely the terms she sets out. In addition, the process
by which she comes to know Christ as "a magnificent prophet"
is itself removed from the trial scene. Sticca points out that a
major tradition surrounding the warning interprets Satan's
intervention as an attempt to rob mankind of salvation by

averting the sacrifice.[19] The verbal borrowings indicate a reliance on Virgil and characterize the scene as a type of pagan
prophecy. As it is presented visually, the mute scene of the
devil with Procula comes close to a parody of the Annuncia-
tion.

The techniques of glossing, multiple acting areas, and
simultaneous action are the principal staging devices of the
Montecassino Passion play. Each of them carries out the re-
orientation of church-drama toward a sense of spectacle. They
allow the playwright both to represent the Passion sequence
and to provide a series of commentaries on the stage action.
These devices also influence the representation of character
in the play. The glossing technique is a means for defining
character. The multiple mansions allow the audience to com-
pare and contrast the personae. With simultaneous staging,
the process can go even further. For example, simultaneous
staging allows the playwright to suggest an equation between
Peter and Judas in the similarities of their laments, yet he can
insist on a difference between them by means of their physical separation on stage.

Like the element of spectacle, the notion of character that
develops in the medieval drama differs sharply from Aristotle's concept. W. H. Auden suggests the difference lies in
assumptions about choice and determinism. He contrasts
Oedipus and Macbeth as representative characters of pagan
Antiquity and Christianity. Oedipus, he says, "has no history,
for there is no relation between his being and his acts. . . . In
Macbeth, on the other hand, every action taken by Macbeth
has an immediate effect upon him so that, step by step, the

19. Sticca, *The Latin Passion Play*, pp. 98–99.

brave bold warrior we hear of in the first scene turns before our eyes into the guilt-crazed creator of the 'tomorrow and tomorrow and tomorrow' soliloquy."[20] Despite remarkable works like *Antigone*, the determinism of classical tragedy tends to invalidate choice as a mark of character. There can be a radical difference between what a man is and what he does. Indeed, Oedipus is the same man after he learns of his crimes that he was when the play began. What has altered is his own awareness that the attempts by him and his parents to thwart the Fates have succeeded only in fulfilling their design. Although Christian drama often deals with divine foreknowledge, its dramatic choices remain a reliable guide to character. Intent figures into each action, and the consequences of choice are knowable and immediate.

The prominence of choice subtly alters the idea of a beginning, middle, and end in drama by making the sequence of these stages responsible to human will. Through the redefinition of spectacle as witnessing, character becomes a more important element. Whereas Aristotle puts the emphasis on plot, Christian drama depicts human action in the face of divine will. Thus the dual purposes that one finds in Aeschylus, Sophocles, and Euripides undergo a transformation as the drama moves from a demonstration of necessity to a depiction of choice. The direction of the change is already apparent in the experiments of Christian writers in late classical Antiquity with narrative "tragedies." Prudentius' *Peristephanon*, X focuses on the will of the martyr Romanus and exhibits the moral choices for which he must account to both civil and divine courts. Since the majority of poems in this collection

20. W. H. Auden, "The Dyer's Hand," *The Listener* 53 (June 16, 1955), 1064.

relate to cult ceremonies for the saints, the aspect of witnessing is brought out even more forcefully.[21] In the fifth century, Dracontius' retelling of the *Oresteia* in his *Orestis tragoedia* uses another trial scene to view questions of choice and responsibility in terms borrowed from Augustine's discussions of determinism and free will.[22]

The major problem the Passion dramatist faces in adapting the element of character to Christian drama lies in portraying Christ. Christ's dual nature would seem to present an insurmountable obstacle to dramatic characterization. As the treatment of Peter indicates, Christ may serve as a model for other characters in the play, but there is no model for him other than the one provided in Scripture. The adumbrations of Christ that medieval commentators find in the Old Testament could offer another approach, but their use by other medieval dramatists only reinforces the difficulty of portrayal. The Anglo-Norman *Jeu d'Adam* lists these Old Testament personnages in its Ordo Prophetarum, and it is scrupulous in its glossing of the characters and figures.[23] For Christ, it uses the term "Figura," much as the Sulmona fragment later turns the "Iesus" of the Cassinese text into "Persona."

The distinction between character and type implied by the other medieval dramas is crucial to the poetics of the Montecassino Passion. The distinction allows one to see two different kinds of effects developed in the play. The first effect can be approached by using Aristotle to gauge the narrative representation of the Passion, for it occurs in time along the gen-

21. See Maurice Cunningham, "The Nature and Purpose of the Peristephanon of Prudentius," *Sacris Erudiri* 14 (1963), 44.
22. Dracontius' reliance on Augustine is discussed by Emanuele Rapisarda, *La Tragedia di Oreste* (Catania: Editore G. Reina, 1951), pp. 193, 215–17.
23. *Le Jeu d'Adam (Ordo representacionis Ade)*, ed. Willem Noomen, Classiques Français du Moyen Age, 99 (Paris: Librairie Champion, 1971), pp. 7–9.

eral outlines of Matthew's gospel. Here characters act out
the broad scheme of the Passion story, and the play's narrative is a spectacle which provides a series of fixed dramatic
situations. Throughout this portrayal Christ remains abstract.
Though his suffering is depicted graphically, he never reacts
to it. He asserts a claim to divinity, yet he never demonstrates
his divine power. Within this series of dramatic situations
there occurs another kind of effect which cannot be approached
in Aristotelian terms; this action is atemporal. Christ as "Persona" represents a defined dramatic situation for Caiaphas,
Peter, and Judas, who must respond to the claim of divinity.
In their responses, they expose their own personalities and
make individual choices which demonstrate varieties of faith
and disbelief. As it depicts these characters, the play carries
out the mystical sense which Rabanus finds in the theater as
the present world where God's servants are held in shame
and made to suffer for the delight of those who wish to remain in a secular world.

These modifications of Aristotelian concepts become immediately apparent in the way the Passion play sets up its
tensions. Christ's speeches reveal the one-dimensional portrait made of him as the central figure of the play. His first
speech, in the betrayal scene, distinguishes the crowd and
Judas as dramatic agents who must react to him. Christ asks:

Why have you come, friend? You have come out with me secretly to
destroy me like a thief. Why did you men not seize me when you used
to see me stand teaching in the temple? Coming with lanterns, weapons, clubs, and lamps, tell me whom you seek.

(vv. 37–45)

The questions are all directed toward the crowd's intentions
and hence emphasize its ability to choose. No clue is provided
for Christ's intention. To achieve this focus on characters

rather than on the figure of Christ, the playwright goes to the model of action in Luke, who is the only evangelist to place the speech to the crowd before the arrest. The sequence of events thus connects the event of the capture to the choices behind it and, by Christ's questions to the soldiers, the playwright allows the crowd to state its mission dramatically and to expose its attitude toward Christ whom they call "the man of innumerable frauds and ghastly faults" (vv. 47–48). In this way, the playwright realizes the social aims of Christian drama. He creates the spectacle of the seizure and, at the same time, illustrates the moral lesson arising from the conflicts between the characters.

In the scenes at Caiaphas' house, the emphasis on character develops from the testimony of the false witnesses, Caiaphas' rage, and Peter's denial to the maid. All these actions are responses to Christ's assertion of divinity and the consequences his divinity will have.

The man you see listening here you will also see coming in heavenly clouds, and you will see the mighty son of God sitting at the right hand of power.

(vv. 88–93)

The glance toward Peter after the denial, which Sticca cites as evidence of the author's stagecraft, continues the stress on character rather than immutable divinity. Peter's flight immediately afterward amounts to yet another reaction to Christ as "Figura." In the scenes with Pilate, Christ maintains this role. Pilate's initial question restates the themes of belief and individual will but reverses the scheme of question and answer. Christ must assert his divinity when Pilate asks, "Are you indeed the king of the Jews? The voices of those who gravely accuse you are numberless" (vv. 160–62). The reversal still permits an illustration of character and moral choice, for Pilate immediately places Christ's answer in contrast to the shouts which it elicits from the priests and soldiers.

The rising action forced by these interchanges heads toward a climax in the trial scenes. The confrontations between antagonists are schematized into two contradictory viewpoints which would seem to require an immediate resolution. The playwright relieves the tension of the rising action by shifting the audience's attention to Procula's chamber. Yet the shift and the introduction of apocryphal material do not modify the essential dramatic situation. Procula has had no contact with Christ in the play, and a demon motivates her affirmation of divinity. In consequence, she can experience Christ only as a figure who involves her in choice and a demonstration of her individual nature. The Crucifixion scene reintroduces the schematized values of the trials. Once again Christ elicits a variety of responses to his divinity from the priests, the thieves, and the Virgin. The priests, now joined by the first thief, retain their disbelief in Christ, while the Virgin and the second thief assert their faith. The extant text provides no clue to the resolution of the play. The modern reader, perhaps like the medieval spectator, views the Crucifixion scene as the final image of the Passion play. He finds dramatic action ending, as it began, with the unique spectacle of sacrifice surrounded by recurrent episodes of moral choice.

The symmetry of the Crucifixion scene reflects the dominant formal arrangement of the Montecassino play and provides an approach to the category Aristotle calls thought (*dianoia*). A system of balance and opposition is pervasive in the work; and each theme, character, or speech is countered by another. Christ directly or indirectly is at the center of these compositions, but the dramatic conflicts are focused in such characters as Peter and Judas. The betrayal provides one example of the composition technique. Viewed schematically, Christ is at the center of the scene. Flanking him are Peter and Judas as spokesmen for the contrary intentions of belief and denial and so as reflections of each other. Beyond them, as the iconography demonstrates, two crowds are pitted against each other in the forms of Caiaphas' retainers and the disciples who later flee the scene. The trial scenes repeat the choice between faith and disbelief, as an opposition between Old and New Laws emerges in the conflict between Caiaphas and Christ; yet to the side of this opposition a reversal takes place. The trial scene includes two groups of witnesses in Peter and those who testify against Christ to Caiaphas. As they claim, the retainers indeed offer "true testimony" in repeating the prophecy about the destruction and rebuilding of the temple (vv. 75–81); they do so, although they do not intend to be prophetic. Carrying out the symmetry and reversal of images, Peter provides false testimony by denying knowledge of Christ to the maid with, ironically, God as his witness: "I call on God as my witness that I do not know the man. I do not know what you are talking about" (vv. 112–14).

The characters of Judas and Peter as well as the techniques of staging further the dramatist's sense of symmetry. In the conspiracy with Caiaphas, Judas immediately exposes the dimensions of his character. He perceives Christ as "the author of deceit" (v. 7), but Caiaphas diminishes Judas from the role of cultural and spiritual guardian to that of a tradesman receiving full payment for goods delivered. To Judas' inflated moral concern for the people, Caiaphas promises that the coins will be of full weight. A similar diminution occurs in the characterization of Peter who in one scene presents himself as Christ's defender and in the next scene denies association with him. The playwright has a basis for the identification of these characters in a tradition which extends back to Cassiodorus' commentary on Psalm 108. Explaining the verse, "May his days be few, and let another take his bishopric," Cassiodorus suggests Peter as the model of the good bishop and finds that "we may know this psalm to be prophetic of the Lord's Passion both from the words of the gospels and the testimony of the apostle Peter. In this verse one must also see the figure of *hypexaeresis*, which is called *exceptio* in Latin: for Judas is excluded from the honor of the bishopric, that is, the apostleship."[24]

In his own age, the playwright could look to the Benedictine abbot Godfrid (c. 1130) who focuses on the close relationship between Judas and Peter in his Palm Sunday homily, "De Samsone et Dalila." Godfrid sees the duality of human nature in Dalila's malevolent character and Samson's fortitude. He offers extended parallels between the Old Testament story and the Passion, likening the cutting of Samson's hair to Christ's flagellation and Samson's frailty to Christ's weakness in Gethsemane. Commenting on the blinding of Samson, he says, "The two eyes of Jesus were the peoples, the Jews and the Gentiles: his two eyes were Adam and Eve, or Peter and Judas. His two eyes, Adam and Eve, were plucked out when Adam, who was the right eye of God did not dread to sin in Paradise. The left eye is torn from him when Eve, who had once looked to God with honest clarity, looked back to the left in listening to the serpent. Christ let the right eye fall when Peter denied him three times in the

---

24. Cassiodorus, *In Psalterium Expositio*, in *Patrologia Latina*, LXX, 785.

The Montecassino Passion

voice of the doorkeeper: he let the left one go when Judas, who betrayed him, hanged himself with a noose."[25]

For a contrasting example of symmetry as *dianoia*, one can look to another twelfth-century play, the *Sponsus* from the abbey of St. Martial at Limoges, which uses balance to structure its total action rather than to connect episodes and characters. The play dramatizes the parable of the Wise and Foolish Virgins (Matthew 25:1–13) who anticipate the arrival of the bridegroom identified as the risen Christ. The Wise Virgins maintain a vigil for Christ, but their foolish sisters sleep too long and spill the oil from their lamps. Asked for help, the Wise Virgins plead for mercy, but Christ consigns their sisters to hell and the devils carry them away immediately. The balance of the scene is not only in the labels Prudentes and Fatuae but also in the refrains associated with each group. The Wise Virgins sing "Gaire noi dormet," while the Foolish Virgins repeat, "Dolentas, Chaitiuas, trop i avem dormit" at the end of each of their five verse stanzas.[26] This formal balance is enhanced by the antiphonal character of the composition. Emile Mâle indicates that the symmetry extends to visual and plastic compositions where the Wise Virgins are placed on Christ's right and the Foolish ones to his left.[27]

St. Jerome's *Commentariorum in Evangelium Matthaei* interprets this symmetry as having to do with contrary intentions and, hence, as an illustration of choice vital to the concept of dramatic character. "We can interpret the five Virgins, the Wise and Foolish ones, as the five senses: some of

25. Godfrid, "Homolia XLII in dominicam in palmis quarta. De Samsone et Dalila (*Judic.* xvi)," in *Patrologia Latina*, CXXXIV, 284.
26. Text in Karl Young, *The Drama of the Medieval Church* (Oxford: Clarendon Press, 1933), II, 362–64.
27. Emile Mâle, *L'art religieux du XIIIᵉ siècle en France: Etude sur l'iconographie du Moyen Age et sur ses sources d'inspiration* (Paris: Thèse pour le doctorat, 1898), p. 259.

184

them hasten toward heaven and desire the celestial; others, longing for the dregs, do not have the balm of virtue with which they might illuminate their hearts."[28] St. Augustine's preaching ("Sermo XCIII") also equates the five virgins with the five senses, and Rabanus continues the tradition, explaining in the *De universo* (vi. 1) "the Wise Virgins can be taken to mean all the holy spirits who, since they admit no corruption of the heart through the five senses of the body, are reckoned for that purpose to be five in number. The five Foolish Virgins are those who have a certain purity of body but do not bear witness to good works in their knowledge, since they glory in their appearance among men but not in their hearts before God."[29] Hugh of St. Victor echoes this view in recognizing the similarities between the Wise and Foolish Virgins in outward form but stressing the intentions of the Wise Virgins to seek "good conscience."[30]

The *Sponsus* emphasizes the transcendent value of its allegory over any empathetic action. Its symmetry continually reveals the alternate choices of the personified figures. To the extent that Christ does intervene in the *Sponsus*, he establishes rewards and punishments for the women and verifies dramatically the wisdom and grace of the Wise Virgins. The symmetry of the Montecassino text differs by treating the characters' choices as more problematic. The Passion play has no system of judgment in its action because the conflict of faith and disbelief remains throughout the play. This open ending contrasts with the treatment that the Passion receives in later medieval drama. The Passion play of the Chester

28. St. Jerome, *Commentariorum in Evangelium Matthaei*, in *Patrologia Latina*, XXVI, 184.

29. St. Augustine, "Sermo XCIII," in *Patrologia Latina*, XXXVIII, 574; Rabanus Maurus, *De universo*, in *Patrologia Latina*, CXI, 79.

30. Hugh of St. Victor, *Allegoriae in Novum Testamentum*, in *Patrologia Latina*, CLXXV, 799.

cycle deals with the issues of belief and denial in the trial
before Annas and Caiaphas which opens the piece. The first
judge says:

> a! Ianglinge Iesu, art thou here?
> now may thou proue thy power,
> whether thy cause be clean and clear,
> thy christhod we shall know.[31]

The witnesses and Caiaphas deny Christ's assertion of divinity, and the sequence of trials before the priests, Pilate,
Herod, and Pilate again develops the issue of faith. Yet the
Chester playwright chooses a particular arrangement to shape
theme and character. He selects episodes that subordinate the
matter of choice to man's redemption through Christ's sacrifice. In these selections, his sense of *dianoia* is close to Aristotle's original connection of thought to rhetorical delivery.

Mary, for instance, achieves an understanding of transcendence in the course of her laments during the Chester play.
She begins the *planctus* with sorrow for the loss of her child
and the sight of his destruction, but other emotions overcome
her grief and she says:

> Alas! the sorrow of this sight
> marrs my mynd, mayne and might,
> but aye my hart me think is light,
> to looke on that I love.

(vv. 649–52)

Christ's speech on the cross further argues transcendence in
the play's action and not merely in its subject matter. In the
Montecassino text, he confronts other characters with a di-
lemma of belief, but in the Chester play he offers statements

<hr>

31. Pageant XVI, vv. 9–12, in *The Chester Plays*, eds. Hermann Deimling
and G. W. Matthews, EETS, ES. no. 115 (1916; rpt. London: Oxford University Press, 1959), II.

of belief and affirmation not in his own divinity but in the
Father's:

> Almighty God in majesty
> to worch thy will I will neuer wand;
> my spirit I betake to thee;
> receiue it, lord, into thy hand!
>
> (vv. 757–60)

The later episodes of the Chester play confirm the almost
didactic explicitness attendant to these choices of belief.
Longeus announces his blindness when Caiaphas orders him
to pierce Christ's heart. The water flowing down the spear
restores the soldier's sight, and in an extended speech he pro-
claims the miracle and his faith in Christ. Joseph of Ari-
mathea finds cause to worship Christ and to glorify his body,
"for we may therwith, perdy, / win vs heaven blisse" (vv.
819–20). Nichodemus recites the catalogue of miracles accompanying the Crucifixion:

> ffor the sonne lost his light,
> Earthqukke made men afright,
> the Roch that never had cleft
> did cleev then, as men might know.
>
> Sepulchrs opened in mens sight,
> dead men rysen ther by night;
> I may say he is god Almight,
> such Signës that can show.
>
> (vv. 877–84)

The emphasis on declamation in these passages shows a treatment of dramatic thought that differs greatly from the treatment in the early Passion play. The Montecassino drama employs balance and symmetry to illustrate the need for moral
choice. The Chester play offers direct instruction in the moral

sense of its action. This overtly didactic approach reflects in turn a different audience with different expectations of the drama.

Perhaps the most readily adapted category of Aristotle's dramaturgy is the element of diction. In the *Poetics*, Aristotle identifies it with meter, though he also points out the connections with rhetoric. The Montecassino author uses diction to complement the dual nature of his work. The regularity of meter imposes a sense of recurrence on the unique events recorded in Scriptural language. Dag Norberg observes that meter tends to modify even the natural differences in the stress patterns of words.[32] *Amarē* and *amāre*, for example, can be used as a rime riche. As diction reshapes the Biblical narrative along new lines, it also makes the dialogue and speeches ideal for musical accompaniment. The trochaic foot, with its initial stress corresponding to the downbeat of Western music, seems especially suited to allow the *ictus* to become the measure of music. In its social implications, meter in the Passion play serves the purpose of meter throughout most of the Middle Ages. It permits the playwright to speak in an impersonal, historical voice and hence to be the spokesman for the community rather than solely for himself.

The playwright's specific approach to diction involves a conscious adaptation of meter. Sticca identifies the meter, the *versus tripartitus caudatus*, with the liturgical sequences of Adam of St. Victor and remarks that "it is not surprising that our unknown dramatist should have chosen for the redaction of his drama the most widely used sequence form of his

32. Dag Norberg, *Introduction à l'étude de la versification latine médiévale* (Stockholm: Almqvist & Wiksell, 1958), p. 117.

Passion Play and Poetics

time."[33] With this popularity there comes as well a set of conventions, and F. J. E. Raby associates the sequence with the elaborate symbolism of the Victorine school.[34] It is here that the playwright would have to adapt the meter to his own requirements. The documentary style of his play generally precludes an elaborate symbolism; the only possible exception is the defective passage where Peter addresses Malchus:

> [S]et [cur] nequam re[t]exosa
> cur verborum venenosa
>   tu sagittas spicula?
> (vv. 53–55)
> But why, wretch, you spiteful thing, why do you shoot
> these deceitful words like poisoned darts?

The use of the sequence apart from the symbolism thus indicates some regard for its recurrent qualities. The verse lends itself particularly to the formal exchanges of dialogue and to set speeches. The form is based on a three-line stanza; it rhymes two lines of eight syllables and ends with a seven-syllable line (*caudatus*) that rhymes with its counterpart in the following stanza. Ferdinand Wolf traces the origin of the *caudatus* to Commodian's hymnody of the third century, yet he observes that the rhyming of final lines is common in folk poetry.[35] There may even be a pedagogical purpose, since meter and rhyme are traditional devices for committing material to memory. The full impact of these modifications in diction lies, however, in their aural effects. The sequence form elevates the paraphrase of Biblical narrative to the level of music.

33. Sticca, *The Latin Passion Play*, p. 61.
34. F. J. E. Raby, *A History of Christian-Latin Poetry*, 2nd ed. (Oxford: Clarendon Press, 1953), pp. 345–75.
35. Ferdinand Wolf, *Über die Lais, Sequenzen und Leiche* (1841; rpt. Osnabrück: Otto Zeller, 1965), pp. 30–32, 198.

The inaccessibility of a work like Aristotle's *Poetics* throughout much of the Middle Ages makes it difficult to analyze the church-drama. The absence of an explicit critical theory forces one to reconstruct a poetics rather than view the works in terms that medieval authors might have used. The difficulty is increased by the breaks between the classical and medieval traditions. Hardison suggests that medieval writers could not have understood classical dramatic criticism even if it had been available. When the text of the *Poetics* was recovered in part through Arabic philosophers, many of its references and its place in Aristotle's corpus were obscured. The central idea of imitation became almost its antithesis, "imaginative representation, . . . the creation of illusion by means of images." Hardison points out this kind of representation is the product of the "imaginative syllogism," "a technique of manipulating language so as to produce the illusion." Another result of the transmission of the text was a reconception of it through rhetorical figures or images. Averroes distorts tragedy into *ars laudandi* and alters its six primary elements. "Plot becomes *sermo fabularis*; character *consuetudines*, a category that includes both actions and morals; thought becomes *credulitas*; diction *metrum*; song *tonus*; and spectacle something called *consideratio*, by which Averroes seems to mean the gestures and facial expressions used by orators to emphasize their arguments."[36]

These changes tend to accord with emphases already apparent in religious drama during the High Middle Ages. The concern with producing illusions finds a counterpart in a dramatic form where spectacle is a major element. The re-

36. O. B. Hardison, Jr., "The Place of Averroes' Commentary on the *Poetics* in the History of Medieval Criticism," in *Medieval and Renaissance Studies*, ed. John L. Lievsay, no. 4 (Durham, N. C.: Duke University Press, 1970), p. 70.

lation of character to moral choice provides another parallel. Hardison indicates that one important distortion of Aristotle was to make "character rather than action the object of imitation" and to intensify "the moral overtones of this revision by making virtue and vice the specific qualities of character to be imitated." Hermannus Alemannus' translation of Averroes' middle commentary on the *Poetics* (1256) reflects these views of the classical genre. Hermannus gave up his own attempt to translate the *Poetics* because the vocabulary was unknown to him.[37] William of Moerbeke did translate the text in 1278, but the work had no apparent influence on contemporary writers.[38]

Although the tradition of dramatic criticism remains isolated, medieval writers never fully lost contact with ancient dramatic works. Mary H. Marshall proposes that some twelfth-century thinkers were familiar with classical theater. "With his great knowledge of Cicero and of his beloved Terence and many other classic authors, John of Salisbury seems to have had a really clear conception of the way in which Roman comedies were performed by gesture and speech."[39] John Scotus, Abelard, Gilbert of La Porée and others follow a Boethian tradition that is based in part on the works of Plautus, Terence, Seneca, and possibly Euripides. Yet their knowledge of the classical tradition is never brought to the church-drama. Even though Abelard's pupil Hilarius was the author of plays on Daniel, Lazarus, and the image of St. Nicholas, the ancient works remain models of style and sources of moral instruction but not paradigms of dramatic

37. *Ibid.*, pp. 69, 64.
38. Guillelmo de Moerbeke, trans., *De arte poetica*, ed. Erse Valgimigli, Aristoteles Latinus, XXXIII (Paris: Desclée de Brouwer, 1953).
39. Mary H. Marshall, "Boethius' Definition of *Persona* and Mediaeval Understanding of the Roman Theater," *Speculum* 25 (1951), 471.

form. Thus the modern critic has to modify some of his approaches and expectations. Above all, he has to devise a method that allows him to see the essential connection between doctrine and aesthetics. In this respect, a work like the Montecassino Passion shows the directions these modifications might take.

Conclusion

THE MONTECASSINO PASSION marks an important innovation in the drama of the Middle Ages. It differs from the traditions of earlier church-drama in several crucial respects. In its subject matter, the play is the first to concentrate on the Passion sequence. In its origin, the play arises from a conscious decision to create a new dramatic form. It is unlike both the liturgical drama that preceded it by two centuries in the West and the dramatized homilies of the Eastern church. Those forms seem to derive from a process of evolution rather than a specific innovation or intentionality. The play's conscious reshaping of the Biblical sources to create a new work brings it instead closer to a form like the cento; as an artist, the playwright has an affinity more to the early Christian writers than to the authors of the liturgical pieces. The poetics underlying the play similarly differs from contemporary notions of the religious drama. The liturgical plays and the kontakia seek to abolish the present moment by reliving Biblical events, but the Passion drama attempts to adapt its form to the nature of its subject. Christian theology treats Christ's suffering and crucifixion as unique and transcendent events in history. The Passion play represents these events while remaining in time and expressing aesthetic and social aims.

The Montecassino Passion

These innovations in the Passion drama make necessary a sequence of trial and error in defining its conventions. The absence of ready models and a critical tradition would force the playwright into a series of experiments. Initially, the experiments center on integrating established forms like law, iconography, and music into the drama. Such integration permits the dramatist several advantages. He can use the established forms to help distinguish his work from the other dramatic modes. Since law, iconography, and music have their own styles of representation, they enforce a distance between the play and its subject matter and point up the aesthetic nature of the piece. These forms also aid the acceptance of the new work by an audience whose expectations of it have not yet been defined. The audience is already familiar with the conventions of the other forms and thus can accept what the playwright attempts in the new genre. Still, the play limits the influence of these borrowings to areas of style, representation, and acceptance. The nature of its topic precludes any larger influence.

The reliance on legal structures is most apparent in the choice of incidents from the Passion accounts. The play is not a Gospel harmony, but it combines the accounts of different evangelists to shape an action that turns on matters of law and contract. Judas' bargain opens the work, and subsequent episodes concentrate on aspects of legal process. The trials before Caiaphas and Pilate occupy the central portion of the play and establish the connection between religious and secular power. The witnesses who appear before these judges provide testimony about Christ's divinity, while the very depiction of the trial scenes characterizes the play as a contemporary document about the Passion. The law also provides a vocabulary for the characters outside the trial scenes. Judas

Conclusion

uses conspicuously legalistic terms in his invective against Christ, and Peter's admission that he denied Christ is phrased in a kind of legal formula.

The documentary style that results from these legal borrowings exists in the context of a larger social preoccupation. The audience would recognize the play's theoretical concerns with transcendence and history as somewhat analogous to its own interests in the Christian past. Earlier pilgrim accounts of the Holy Land had been transcribed, and new works were being composed from those sources during the period. The aim of this documentary activity is to devise means for recovering time and space imaginatively. By allegorical identifications with the Biblical past and historical analogies to earlier ecclesiastical forms, the playwright's contemporaries seek models for defining the nature of social life. The process extends beyond literary compositions to efforts at restoring the basilica of St. Benedict, the acquisition of relics, and the incorporation of ancient ceremonies and rituals. The play's aesthetics of recovery thus finds support in the general movement toward a Christian antiquarianism.

Much as the dramatist shapes the action of his new work around legal process, he defines its visual qualities by analogues in the pictorial arts. In some cases, this reliance seems so strong that the play appears to follow the conventions of iconography in preference to the details in the Biblical sources. From the artists, the playwright would learn how to arrange the staging of his action. By the sixth century, miniaturists are able to portray multiple and simultaneous action, and their works are known and imitated in southern Italy soon afterward. Byzantine miniature sequences in particular would contain models for the visual features of the Passion drama. These models not only show how to direct the action of the play but also suggest how the images could represent in concrete form the transcendent events of the Gospels. To an extent, the play follows the lines of a miniature cycle. The impact of the iconographical images is so great that the drama assumes the iconic style of the miniatures and accepts the visual artists' own accommodations to a static medium by using the devices of condensation, conflation, and omission.

To regain the sense of movement natural to drama and strengthen the transcendent element even more, the dramatist recurs to yet another established form. The element of music is the bridge between the discrete actions of the episodes. It establishes a continuity against which the fragmented, iconic action can be placed and acts as an interlude between scenes. It can even accelerate or retard action as needed. In addition, music adds another dimension to the flow of narrative and dramatic action. As a mirror of universal order, it connects the play's spectacle and visual qualities to literal, moral, and anagogic truth. The nature of this relation allows one, in turn, to distinguish the Passion play from liturgy. As an autonomous form, liturgy enlists belief but is not created or validated by successive acts of faith. Medieval and modern thinkers stress that it remains in a timeless world of symbols and types, encompassing and entering history, whereas drama has a time-centered world which it aims to escape. The Passion play exists on a histrionic level, but liturgy claims to present a genuine reenactment instead of a mimetic crucifixion. Thus the emergent genre limits its reliance on aspects of church ritual. Without attempting to duplicate the Mass or the divine offices, the dramatist shares themes from liturgy and uses worship as a context for the new work.

The dual nature of the Passion play suggests that modern

criticism has to modify some of its approaches to the early medieval drama. The doctrinal values attached to the subject matter of the Montecassino play align it more with the Platonism of the twelfth century than with the Aristotelianism of the thirteenth. The categories that Aristotle sets down in the *Poetics* undergo redefinition and reversal. They remain useful to the critic for understanding the recurrent features of the drama but not its central ideological focus. The majority of dramatic writing in the Middle Ages continued in the directions of the Montecassino Passion. The incorporation of apocryphal material and the tendency toward episodic structure become characteristic of the English Corpus Christi cycles. Those cycles, which conceived their diverse episodes as parts of a single play, add an allegorical dimension to the issues of character and choice that the Montecassino play treats individually. Yet in such modifications the English cycles maintain a linear view of history by beginning with a Creation play and progressing historically through the Old and New Testaments toward the Last Judgment. On the continent, the great mystery plays of the later Middle Ages refine the aesthetic possibilities of spectacle in their extravagant productions and machines. These possibilities continued to engage experimenters and theorists of the drama throughout the Renaissance.

Index

Abelard, 191
Acta Pilati, 33, 115, 117. *See also* Procula
Adam of St. Victor, 188–189
Adamnanus, 70
Aeschylus: Aristotle on, 58; *Prometheus Bound*, 160; dual purposes in, 177
Agonotheta, 49
Alan de Lille, 164
Allen, Philip S., 60–61
Alphanus, 65–66, 96
Amalarius of Metz, 47–48, 50, 55–56, 132, 151–152
Antiquarianism, Christian, 5, 66, 67–72, 81, 84, 195
Apel, Willi, 151
Apuleius, 63
Aristotle: Aristotelian criticism, 7, 55, 57–58; on spectacle, 8, 160; modified Aristotelian approach, 159–160, 176–179, 196–197; on *dianoia*, 181, 186; on diction, 188; *Poetics* in Middle Ages, 190–191
Ars dictaminis, 30
Attitudes toward drama, 4, 57, 160–162; toward classical drama, 190–192
Auden, W. H., 176
Audience, 6, 53–55, 59, 66, 69, 74, 85, 162–163, 167, 174

Auerbach, Erich, 62
Augustine, Saint, 4, 128, 138, 141–142, 143, 145, 185
Averroes, 190, 191

Bachelard, Gaston, 72, 73
Basilica: acting in, 44, 54; reconstruction of St. Benedict under Desiderius, 74–77, 96
Baumstark, Anton, 132, 133, 136–137
Bede, 67–71 *passim*
Bernard, Saint, 161
Bevington, David, 22
Bloch, Herbert, 74
Boethius, 128, 191
Book of Cerne, 45–46
Bristol Psalter, 99

Caedmon, 130
Cargill, Oscar, 35
Carpenter, Marjorie, 40
Casel, Dom Odo, 125
Cassiodorus, 183
Cento, 44–46, 193
Chambers, E. K., 43
Character, 176–181; of Christ in Passion play, 178–181; of Peter and Judas, 182–184; in Averroes, 190–191

199

Index

Chester, 83; Passion play, 171, 185–188

Chludoff Psalter, 100, 104.

Christos Paschon, 43–44

Cicero, 49, 191

Codex Purpureus Rossanensis, 99, 103, 114, 115–117, 120

Cohen, Gustave, 173

Commodian, 189

Comparetti, Domenico, 44

Constantine, 77, 89, 126

Cyprus Passion Cycle, 95–96

Davidson, Clifford, 36

De Bartholomaeis, Vincenzo, 24

Der Nersessian, Sirarpie, 92

Desiderius, 23, 74–75, 76–77, 85, 96

Determinism, 33, 177, 178

Dianoia, 181–188; in Averroes, 190

Diction, 188–189; in Averroes, 190

Dix, Gregory, 124, 132, 137

Document: play as, 25, 52; documentary style, 54, 62–63, 95, 97, 189

Dracontius, 32–33, 178

Dream of the Rood, 61

Duchesne, Léopold, 133

Dumville, David N., 45

Dunn, E. Catherine, 129

Else, Gerald, 83

Eucharistia, 126, 132–134

Euripides, 43, 177, 191

Eusebius, 63, 127

Every, George, 75–76

Exultet roll, 107, 108

Flanigan, C. Clifford, 38

Fleming, John V., 164

Fortunatus, 60–61

Frank, Grace, 172–173

Friend, Jr., A. M., 124

Gallican Rite, 50, 154

Gelasius, Pope, 45

Gilbert of La Porée, 191

Glossing, 163–170, 171–172, 176

Gnosticism, 126

Godfrid, Abbot, 183–184

Goetz, Georg, 164

Grabar, André, 92, 93, 123–124, 126, 168

Gratian, 31

Gregory the Great, Pope, 84, 88, 90, 92, 123

Gregory Nazianzenus, 43, 44, 92

Gregory of Nyssa, 87, 89–90

Guardini, Romano, 125, 130, 142

Gutkind, C. S., 24

Hardison, Jr., O. B., 47, 48, 49, 58, 140, 143–144, 150, 151–152, 156, 160, 190, 191

Hatch, William, 119

Herbert, J. A., 93, 94, 119

Hermannus Alemannus, 191

Hilarius, 191

Hippolytus of Rome, 134, 137

Honorius of Autun, 48–50, 132

Hortus Deliciarum, 118

Hrotswitha of Gandersheim, 51

Hugh of St. Victor, 185

Iliad, 91

Images: in kontakia, 4; repetition in 36; of earlier religious communities, 78–80, 84–85; defense of, 87–90, 123; powers of, 89–90, 93; book illustrations as, 91–92; informative and expressive, 168; iconic, 170; imaginative syllogism, 190

Imitation: text as, 8; cultic, 37–38; dramatic different from liturgical, 39; in Benediktbeuern Passion play, 52–54; liturgical, 55–56; in linear time, 59; in ceremonies, 78–83; and audience, 165; distortion by Averroes, 190

Index

Inguanez, Dom Mauro, 12n, 22, 23, 24, 96–97, 98
Isidore of Seville, 4

Jerome, Saint, 184–185
Jeu d'Adam, 157, 178
Jodogne, Omer, 162
John of Salisbury, 191
John Scotus, 191
Judas: representations of bargain, 97–102; representations of betrayal, 102–106; representations of repentance, 113–115, 120; connected to Barabbas in Good Friday liturgy, 143; repentance scene in Passion play, 174–175; equated with Peter, 176
Jung, Carl G., 132
Jungmann, Josef A., 126, 134, 138, 139
Justinian: *Instituta, Novella, Codex*, 31; *Digesta Justiniana*, 49

Kitzinger, Ernst, 87, 89–90
Kontakia, 4, 39–44, 140; different from liturgical drama, 42–43

La Piana, Giorgio, 40–41, 139–140
Laurenziana Gospels, 99, 100, 110, 111, 114
Law: incorporation in Passion play, 26–31, 194–195; legal description, 26, 27, 68, 98; customary law, 28, 50; Roman law, 30–31, 49; legal writing at Montecassino, 30–31; trial in Prudentius, 32–33, 177; trial in Dracontius, 32–33, 178; trial before Caiaphas, in art, 110–113, in Passion play, 164–166, 182; trial before Pilate, in art, 115–119, in Passion play, 180–181; trial in Chester Passion play, 186. See *also* Testimony
Leo Marsicanus, 30, 75

Leon, Harry J., 67
Leuterman, Teodoro, 135, 138, 139, 147, 148, 151–152, 156
Lévi-Strauss, Claude, 73
Liturgical drama, 4, 34–39; *quem queritis* trope, 34–39 *passim*, 58; trope not dramatic, 35; different from kontakia, 42–43; and visual arts, 86. See *also* Kontakia
Liturgy: different from drama, 6, 123, 140–141, 196; Roman Rite, 79, 133, 137, 138; Jerusalem Church, 79, 136–137, 138, 152; Mandatum, 79, 82; Sermo Dominicus, 82–83; attitudes toward liturgy, 125–126, 130–132; Antioch Church, 129, 137; early development of liturgy, 132–135; Cathedral Rite, 132, 134–137; Monastic Rite, 132, 137–141; Montecassino Ordo, 134–135, 155–156; centralized liturgy, 134–135, 136–137; Roman Ordines, 135, 138, 151, 152, 154; Adoratio crucis, 136, 138, 152–157; influence of Byzantine liturgy, 138, 141; Alexandrian Church, 138; themes in liturgy, 138–140, 141, 144–147, 148, 150, 156–157; Byzantine liturgy, 139–140; Good Friday liturgy, 141–157; ritual action, 147, 148–149, 150–156; Einsiedeln Ordo, 152; *improperia*, 153–156; liturgy and later drama, 157. See *also* Liturgical drama; Kontakia
Liutprand, 139
Loerke, William, 116–117
Lowe, E. A., 94

Macbeth, 176–177
Mahr, August, 95
Mâle, Emile, 86, 184
Marcus Victorinus, 44
Marshall, Mary H., 191

Index

Martianus Capella, 128
Masai, François, 91
Millet, Gabriel, 103–104, 107
Miniature: in narrative descriptions, 70, 72–73; in MS of Passion play, 96–97
Mnemonics, 72
Momigliano, Arnaldo, 63
Music: incorporation into drama, 6, 123, 157–158, 196; Gregorian chant, 35; repetition through, 36; place in liturgy, 124, 126–131, 149; theory, 128–129, 130–131; responsorial singing, 129; antiphonal singing, 129–130; Ambrosian chant suppressed, 134–135; standardization in eleventh century, 135–136; treatises at Montecassino, 136; character of Byzantine, 139; Trisagion, 153, 155, 156; influence of Byzantine, 155–156
Mystère de la Passion, 61

Neoplatonism, 90, 130, 159
Neri, Francesco, 23
Newton, Francis, 12n., 45
Norberg, Dag, 188
Northern Passion, 60

Pacht, Otto, 86, 121
Panofsky, Erwin, 79–80
Passion de Clermont-Ferrand, 60
Passion des jongleurs, 60
Passion lyrics, 60–61
Passion plays: in *Carmina Burana*, 22; *Ludus breuiter de passione*, 33; late appearance of, 46–47; *Ludus de passione*, 52–53; *Mystère de la Passion*, 61; York play, 166–167; Chester play, 171, 185–188. See also Sulmona fragment
Paul, Saint, 7, 160, 161, 162
Peregrinatio Egeriae, 63, 67–69, 81–82, 137, 152, 156
Peter: representations of attack on

Malchus, 104–106, 108, 120; representations of denial of Christ, 111–113; glossing in attack on Malchus, 164; denial of Christ in Passion play, 169–170; characterization in Passion play, 171 174–175; equated with Judas, 176
Peter the Deacon, 69, 70–72, 76–77
Philo of Alexandria, 127
Planctus, 22, 24, 54–55, 135, 139, 163; *Planctus ante nescia*, 23; lyric elements in 61; in Chester Passion play, 186
Plautus, 191
Pliny the Younger, 3
Pomponius, 44
Proba Faltonia, 44
Procula, 33, 117–119, 171, 175–176, 181. See also *Acta Pilati*
Prudentius, 32–33, 96n., 177–178

Quintillian, 164

Rabanus Maurus, 4, 76, 161–162, 185
Rabula Gospels, 104
Raby, F. J. E., 189
Registrum I Thomae Abbatis 1285–1288, 22
Regula Monachorum, 79, 82–83, 138
Regularis Concordia, 36–38, 59
Reinhold, H. A., 132
Relics, 78, 89–90, 150
Repetition: in liturgical drama, 4, 36; in Aristotle, 7, 55; in *Regularis Concordia*, 59; in *Peregrinatio Egeriae*, 68–69; of themes in liturgy, 141; in staging techniques, 163, 169–170, 172; recurrence in moral choice, 181; in diction, 188, 189
Ritmus in Laudem Montis Casini, 64–65
Romanos, 41–42, 130
Romanus, martyr. *See* Prudentius

Index

Rossano Gospels. See *Codex Purpureus Rossanensis*
Rubrics, 8, 87, 162, 165–168
Rudick, Michael, 52–53
Rufinus, 63

Saint Augustine Gospels, 105, 110
Salter, F. M., 83
Sant'Apollinare Nuovo, 103, 104, 110, 111, 112, 114, 117
Sant'Angelo in Formis, 96, 108, 118
Sedulius, 44
Seneca, 191
Sepet, Marius, 58
Smiley, Marilynn, 135–136
Smoldon, William L., 35–36
Sophocles, 177; Oedipus, 176–177; *Antigone,* 177
Sophronios, 155
Space: transformation in drama, 59–62; Montecassino as Mount Sinai, 64–66, 67, 84, 149; in antiquarian writing, 67–74, 85; Jerusalem as *axis mundi,* 175
Spectacle, 7, 8, 159–163, 164–165, 173, 176, 177, 180; in Averroes, 190
Spitzer, Leo, 68
Sponsus, 157, 184–185
Staging: in basilica, 44, 54; in miniatures, 113, 114, 120; in liturgy, 148–149; techniques in Passion play, 162–170; multiple mansion, 170–172; simultaneous, 172–176
Stephen IX, Pope, 94, 134
Sticca, Sandro, 43, 44, 50, 51, 96, 115, 162, 170–171, 175, 180, 188
Stuttgart Psalter, 110–111, 112
Sulmona fragment, 2, 22, 171, 178
Synaxis, 133, 140, 141

Tacitus, 63
Taylor, Jerome, 57
Terence, 51, 52, 63, 191
Tertullian, 4, 54, 160–161, 162

Testimony, 27–32 *passim,* 164; and glossing, 182; play as, 165
Thucydides, 63
Time: uniqueness of events in Christian, 2, 7–8, 39, 52, 58–59, 131, 137–138; aesthetic forms in, 47; depiction in, 114, 120–121, 178–180. See also Repetition
Toschi, Paolo, 24, 162
Tragicus, 48, 49, 54
Transcendence: of Passion, 2, 58–59, 193; through iconography, 3, 5, 87–90, 92–93, 95–96, 119–120; through music, 3, 126–131, 157–158; related to antiquarianism, 5, 62–63, 66, 195; and liturgy, 6, 47, 123, 125, 141; in drama, 8, 39, 51–52, 56, 159, 163, 168, 186; basilica as image of, 75–76

Ummidia Quadratilla, 3

Varro, 63, 66
Versus tripartitus caudatus, 104, 188–189
Virgil, 44; *Aeneid,* 33–34, 91, 98
Visual arts, 5–6; iconography, 71, 168; and drama, 86–122, 195–196; iconography and dramatic technique, 87, 119–22; Byzantine art, 87, 123–124; iconoclasm, 88, 91; book illustration, 90–95; Byzantine decoration, 93; Byzantine art and Cyprus Passion Cycle, 95–96; at Montecassino, 96. See also Images; Miniature

Wakefield Master, 61–62
Watkin, E. I., 80
Weitzmann, Kurt, 120, 121
Wellesz, Egon, 139, 156
Whitrow, G. J., 58
Wickham, Glynne, 83–84, 172
William of Moerbeke, 191
Witke, Charles, 32

Wolf, Ferdinand, 189
Woolf, Rosemary, 88, 130, 161
Wormwald, Francis, 105

York Crucifixion pageant, 166–167
Young, Karl, 24, 34–35, 43, 46–47, 52, 152